FINDING GOD IN THE SHADOWS

FINDING GOD IN THE SHADOWS

Stories from the Battlefield of Life

Marsha Hansen

&

Peter A. Huchthausen

Augsburg Books

Minneapolis

FINDING GOD IN THE SHADOWS
Stories from the Battlefield of Life

Cover design: Danielle Carnito
Cover photo © Nat Farbman/Time & Life Pictures/Getty Images. Used by permission.
Book design: Michelle L. N. Cook

Library of Congress Cataloging-in-Publication Data
Hansen, Marsha, 1952–
Finding God in the shadows : stories from the battlefield of life / by Marsha Hansen and Peter Huchthausen.
    p. cm.
ISBN 978-0-8066-5326-6 (alk. paper)
1. Christian life. I. Huchthausen, Peter A., 1939- II. Title.
BV4515.H3185 2007
248.4–dc22
2007028119

12   11   10   09   08   1   2   3   4   5   6   7   8   9   10

Contents

Introduction

This book is designed to help those who wish to practice what the prophet Micah taught: God's will is that we do justice, love mercy, and walk humbly before our God. Here you will find the stories of men and women facing imperfect choices in difficult and dangerous situations—people who exhibit moral courage despite hardships, privations, and the burden of making life and death decisions for others.

The stories are all true and are set in the context of war: World War II, the Vietnam War, and the Cold War. Many of the stories recount extreme situations in desperate times; however, our intent in telling them is not to offer a theology of war, but rather to examine issues of faith and ethics through the experiences of people whose lives have been touched and changed by crises.

Each story is followed by a reflection that sets the characters and their tale against biblical events that illuminate modern realities. This is not an exercise in biblical theology; it is simply the juxtaposition of ancient and modern stories in such a way that they shed light on each other and draw out common themes of justice, love, and mercy—themes that motivated, and continue to motivate, people of faith in their struggle to be faithful to the God who has called them. By searching the ordinary realities within which many people of the Bible encountered and attempted to serve God, we intend both to encourage a closer reading of the scriptures and to create a framework for thinking more deeply about the stories in this book. Against the background of Scripture, it does not matter that the stories in this book are primarily war stories. Regrettable though it is, war is a reality in human history, and the experiences of people in war can be instructive for the rest of us. What we hope to demonstrate in this book is the fact that, regardless of life circumstances (including war), all of life spins around one central question for each person: "Will I see the image of God in others and let this guide what I think, what I feel, what I say, and what I do?"

The author of these stories, Peter Huchthausen, writes that they are experiences taken from the "great odyssey of life." No one account is extraordinary and yet, as a whole, the stories represent a very human panorama of events—events with the power to shape vision and compel courageous action, events with the power to leave lifelong memories and lifelong scars. Most of the characters depicted were not heroes in the true sense of the word, but were rather ordinary people whose life experiences confronted them with difficult choices in difficult circumstances. Their experiences—and the experiences of the ancient Hebrews also told here—might well inform the way we go about making our own choices. These reflections cover a wide spectrum of faith concerns, and it is our hope that you will find here a framework for asking—and answering—critical questions about common human dilemmas.

In his *Letters and Papers from Prison*, German theologian Dietrich Bonhoeffer wrote of the "responsible man who tries to make his whole life an answer to the question and call of God."[1] Two of Bonhoeffer's questions with respect to such moral responsibility are relevant to the stories you are about to read: "Is God's love any less for our enemies, for whom God just as much came, suffered, and died, as God did for us?" and "Who stands fast?"[2] These are questions for the difficult places in life. May they guide your reading.

    —Marsha Hansen
      Author of the Biblical Reflections

CHAPTER 1

The Battle of Pilar Pass

My father served as an army chaplain during World War II, and while assigned to an infantry regiment saw a great deal of close ground combat against the Japanese in New Guinea and the Philippines. After the war he remained in the army, serving as a Lutheran chaplain.

As I grew up, and our family traveled from one army post to another, Dad rarely spoke of the war. Occasionally, however, when he was moved by some event in his daily round of counseling soldiers and looking after the spiritual well-being of his assigned unit or post, he would relate anecdotes of his days on the battlefield. One of his stories in particular has stayed with me—I heard it as a sermon illustration many times.

During the liberation of the Philippines, Dad was assigned to the First U.S. Infantry Regiment, the oldest infantry unit of the U.S. Army. The regiment landed in Lingayen Gulf with the Sixth Infantry Division in January 1945, and, through three months of harrowing combat, fought its way to Manila.

The Japanese military code of *Bushido* did not exempt medical and religious soldiers as targets. Medics and chaplains wore an identifying red cross on a white armband; nevertheless they were targeted by snipers and were urged by their regimental officers to carry side arms in self-defense.

The Japanese soldier, however, was also guided by a code called *Senjinkun,* which was spelled out in a field manual distributed to every Japanese soldier in January 1941 by order of Prime Minister General Hideki Tojo. The code was intended to prevent a recurrence of the massacres of the early years of the war, such as in Nanking, China. Although compiled predominantly by senior army officers, the code included the views of prominent Japanese university professors and even a poet.

Despite its intention to prevent further misconduct on the battlefield, the code in effect became a primer for further Japanese militarism. The code explicitly stated that a soldier was bound by the honor of his name never to suffer the disgrace of capture. The code stated that the soldier was to "always retain the spirit of attack and always maintain freedom of action. Never give up your position, but rather die." The code did not address conduct toward noncombatants or civilians, hence the Japanese seemed to totally disregard the welfare of civilians on or near the battlefield.

In contrast, the American fighting man was governed by traditional American benevolence and by the rules of warfare as stated in the 1929 Geneva Conventions. Further, the U.S. military generally operated with a notion of fair play when it came to civilians, and usually acted within the boundaries of a common understanding of morality that exempted unarmed civilians from attack.

During the long hard fight to liberate Manila, Dad's regiment took part in what came to be known as the battle of the Pilar Pass. On February 1, the First Infantry was sent to augment the Eleventh Corps, which had run into heavy Japanese resistance to their advance on the infamous Bataan Peninsula. The regiment began its attack near the town of Orani and, after a full day of advancing, approached the ridge near the town of Pilar.

That night the regiment was attacked by a force of about three hundred Japanese, and for the next week heavy combat raged in the battle of Pilar Pass. The fighting grew particularly vicious during the third day with the front line shifting precariously and both sides suffering heavy casualties.

At one point the line stabilized along a major east-west road with Japanese infantry dug in on one side and the advancing Americans on the other. Dad described repeated and harrowing Japanese *banzai* attacks by hordes of infantry emerging from the tree line to the south. The Japanese threw themselves without hesitation into the American lines on the other side of the road using bayonets and hand grenades. The attacks often began early in the morning or in the shadows of twilight when visibility was limited and it was difficult to discern friend from foe. The road was littered with the dead and wounded as the fighting continued for two days and nights.

Late one afternoon, as the shooting diminished, Dad and his fellow troops observed a young Filipino girl, about eight years of age, staggering down the road where the hill leveled off near the center of the worst fighting of the previous days. Several of the infantrymen dug in by Dad watched in horror as the girl, crying and bleeding from several wounds, neared the main lines. Sporadic fire gradually ceased from the American side and the men watched helplessly as the girl approached certain disaster.

For a while, Japanese snipers continued to shoot into the American lines. One soldier near Dad swore audibly and began to leave the protection of his position. He was cautioned first and then ordered to get down by his platoon sergeant. The young soldier was deeply distressed and, like many of the others observing the approaching girl, was determined to take action to prevent her from wandering into the center of the most hotly contested area. As a result of fatigue, or just the urge to do something after the long and seemingly endless hours of chaos, shelling, and heavy machine-gun fire, the young soldier was ready to act.

Dad, observing the distress of the anxious soldier and hearing the shouts of the platoon sergeant to stay put, rolled toward the man to comfort him. Dad explained that all those present wanted to do something to save the girl, but the enemy would certainly not permit any approach from the side of the road to help her. It would be suicide to try. The well-being of the entire unit was at stake and he must obey the orders of his superior.

As Dad struggled to contain the young rifleman, it suddenly became eerily quiet and they realized that the Japanese had also stopped firing. All watched in silence as the girl continued to approach the entrenched positions, walking down the center of the road crying.

The sudden quiet apparently galvanized the courage of the young soldier. He shook off all attempts at restraint, stood up, dropped his weapon, and walked into the center of the road in plain view of both sides. He scooped the terrified young girl into his arms and walked back to the rear of the lines. The silence continued until the soldier and girl were out of view and then the firing resumed. The soldier was never reprimanded for disobeying orders—neither was he ever rewarded for what he did.

Urgent need in times of human crisis, when life hangs on the edge and death stares one in the face, can strip away one's sense of fear, replacing it with the desire to do something meaningful and worthwhile in the face of all the carnage and chaos. It is said that there are no atheists in foxholes, but whatever the inspiration that runs through a man or woman at such times, it is surely a sign that there is a greater good that breathes in all of us, and that in some of us it can overpower our normal reaction of self-preservation.

Stories of unmatched courage on the battlefield, during natural calamities, accidents, or other adversities demonstrate that the urge to do the right thing, to take a risk on the side of goodness, to try to accomplish something positive burns in most humans, whatever their faith or lack of faith. This desire to do what's right seems particularly strong when men and woman are witness to large-scale carnage and loss of life. Great human loss may at times seem to render all life as tentative and futile. On the other hand, such tremendous human loss often leads people to focus on the value of each individual life and the importance of survival.

One need only read the accounts of medics and hospital corpsmen who perform incredible acts of selfless sacrifice and bravery just to save one individual life while around them others are falling in large numbers. It may be intrinsic to the human spirit that, when suffering seems universal and becomes nearly overpowering, we cling to the notion that every life is important and worth trying to preserve.

Biblical Reflection

The wolf shall live with the lamb, the leopard shall lie down with the kid, the calf and the lion and the fatling together, and a little child shall lead them. Isaiah 11:6

Can there be hope in the middle of chaos and destruction? Can the will toward sacrificial love drive men and women to act selflessly in times of crisis? "The Battle of Pilar Pass" is a powerful story that inspires such hope while raising questions about what drives and shapes our ethical choices and actions. What factors determine who we will become and how we will act? What circumstances might circumvent our acting in accord with our own moral sense and spirituality? In times of crisis, when death looms large for others or ourselves, how do we make the decisions that we do, and what do those decisions say about us and our regard for life?

Sustained crises, particularly wars, inevitably change people at some level. Yet there seems to be a spirit of rebellion within each of us demanding that, in spite of the crisis, our individual existence must continue to stand for the things we most value. In war this notion often takes a beating. People individually and collectively are gripped by stresses, dangers, and tensions imposed on them by powerful external forces over which they seem to have no control.

The forces of war sweep us in directions that are frequently in conflict with what we would normally choose for ourselves. In the normal course of living we are not disposed to outfit ourselves or our sons and daughters with guns, grenades, and other instruments of destruction, nor do we prepare to encamp in foreign battlefields—or any battlefield for that matter. Our normal inclinations are toward fruitful work and the fulfillment of life goals that bring personal meaning to our routine tasks, tasks we prefer to choose for ourselves.

War is an aberration, regardless of whether the motive for engaging others in the fray is containment, liberation, or aggression. Throughout history, people have accepted war as a necessary evil. Tales of large-scale mortal conflict are recorded in the earliest writings of most world cultures. To stand and fight has often been necessary simply to preserve life when other measures have failed.

Today our enemies are likely to be people whom we know little about and with whom we have had little direct contact. Their values, religious expressions, and ways of life in general are likely to be quite different from our own experiences. Nevertheless, like the American and Japanese infantrymen battling at Pilar Pass in the Philippines, people from radically different cultures and circumstances are tossed into battle not as individuals, but as armies. In close combat they face and inflict mortal harm as individuals, but at the same time act as a unit—the collective character of which often shapes and controls the behavior of the individuals who wear its uniforms.

An army of warriors functions as a unified organism as opposed to a mere collection of individual soldiers. The aftermath of their battles is viewed objectively in terms of the number of troops lost, ground gained, lines held. It is only later that we sort out the dead, account for individuals, shed tears, and count the many costs. This is war.

In the story of Pilar Pass, some central questions about war emerge, two of which are very important: can an army have character, and what characterizes one army from another? The Japanese military codes of *Bushido* and *Senjinkun* and the Geneva Conventions present radically different ideas as to the proper conduct of war. The Geneva Conventions address the treatment of noncombatants and civilians, while the *Senjinkun*, a modern interpretation and distillation of elements from the ancient unwritten code of *Bushido*, does not. Even though each Japanese soldier was equipped with a copy of the *Senjinkun* code, whose stated intention was to prevent barbarity, barbarity was not prevented. Why? Because the primary emphasis of the *Senjinkun* code was on the efficient execution of war, on the honor of the soldier and his resolve to fight to the death, and not on the humane treatment of the inevitable noncombatant victims of war.

Even though such laudable virtues as courage, benevolence, respect, honor, loyalty, and honesty are central tenets of *Bushido,* the ancient way of the warrior, these virtues did not extend to treatment of the enemy. Despite certain Zen elements in *Bushido,* and despite the opposition among some Zen Buddhist leaders to the growth of Japanese militarism, increasing military aggression was actually encouraged by *Senjinkun.*

Let's consider what happened at Pilar Pass when one side fought under the militaristic philosophy enshrined in *Senjinkun* and the other under the Geneva Conventions. Innocence came walking down the road between opposing armies, wounded, bleeding, lost, alone, and crying. A small girl appeared in the midst of a heated battle. While grown men held each other at bay and jockeyed for position with lethal force, battered life wandered in misery into the teeth of near certain annihilation.

What sane person wants to see life annihilated? First the Americans ceased firing, and then, remarkably, so did the Japanese. Perhaps this surprised the American forces who understood the Japanese commitment to wage war to the death of the very last soldier.

What happened within the silence, when the guns ceased firing? We are told the story of two men, the distressed soldier and the chaplain who struggled to comfort him. We hear in the chaplain's counsel that many other soldiers felt a burden for the young girl as well. No doubt this burden fell on the men on both sides of the fighting. No doubt one little, wounded girl presented an image of life so strongly to all the men present that day that all were compelled to stop firing in the hope that perhaps she would turn back, in the hope that it would not be their bullet that felled her and brought her final moments.

Yet for one soldier, even when it was pressed upon him that to attempt a rescue would be tantamount to suicide and would be futile for him and the little girl, something compelled him to throw down his weapon in the sight of his enemies and do what they all wanted—save an innocent life. The compelling force that moved the soldier to action is the force of sacrificial love that permeates the spirits of those who have a deep sense of the sanctity of life. With nothing at all to shield him except his own need to affirm the life of a child—and thereby to affirm life itself—he risked all to go to the girl, to lift her up, and to carry her in his arms, her little body shielded by his body.

At the moment he lifted her up and no bullets flew, his individual effort became the collective effort of all the men present that day—both American and Japanese—to do good. It was a moment of recognition that said "yes" to the image of God in all of us, even when we are engaged in combat or conflict. This demonstration of the willingness to affirm life under the most extreme circumstances carries a strong message that clearly cuts across cultural lines.

Judeo-Christian scriptures tell us that there is one creator and that all human beings are created in the image of God. Sometimes, when confronted with the masses of humankind, we fail to see this image, but when one lone, defenseless innocent wanders down the road in our direction and depends upon us to see the image of God present within her, that image shines in a way that can light any darkness. The image of God in others speaks softly but with such force that those who bear the image of God within themselves are moved to respond with love in action no matter the cost.

CHAPTER 2

Stalingrad

I n July 1989, the year following the historic Moscow summit and just months prior to the fall of the Berlin Wall, the Soviet defense ministry allowed U.S. and West German naval attachés to book a tour boat down the Volga River from Kazan', east of Moscow, to Stalingrad (known today by its historical name of Volgograd). The two-week tour was for Westerners only and was comprised primarily of German passengers.

The journey began on the wide confluence where the Kama River joins with the Volga before the latter swells out and flows majestically toward Ul'yanovsk, the birthplace of Vladimir Lenin. On its journey, the boat would pass through a section of the river that had been closed for more than six decades to foreigners and nonresident Soviet citizens due to the presence of defense industries. The tour would terminate in Rostov on Don just north of the Black Sea.

Aboard as tourists were twelve German veterans of the ill-fated Wehrmacht Sixth Army, which had fought the long and bloody Battle of Stalingrad from June 1942 to February 1943, only to end in defeat and surrender. More than 800,000 Axis soldiers died, while the Red Army lost about one million men and women. Civilian losses were estimated as 300,000. Of more than 91,000 Germans taken prisoner, few survived, and many of those who did returned to Germany only late in the 1950s.

After reaching Stalingrad six days into the trip, the boat docked on the Volga's west bank across from high bluffs overlooking a wide swell as the river made a sharp turn to the east. A young German-speaking Russian Intourist guide led the curious and solemn German veterans on a tour of the city, parts of it still in ruins as a memorial to the heavy loss of life. The two Moscow-based naval attachés accompanied the veterans on the city tour.

The first stop on the tour was in Mamaya Kurgan on the outskirts of the city. There atop a lonely hill loomed the larger-than-life statue of Mother Russia, arms outstretched, sword in hand, looking fiercely eastward, daring those present to forget the hundreds of thousands who died in the city. The guide recited her rote script in stilted German, accenting time and again the number of Russian military and civilians killed by the Nazi armies. The German veterans listened in stoic silence. Several of the veterans were missing limbs; most sported scars visible in their light clothing in the hot and humid Russian summer.

After visiting many parts of the town, the tour made a final stop at the Red Army museum located near the famous Dzerzhinsky tractor factory, where some of the heaviest fighting had taken place. Many buildings still stood as in 1943, in shambles, some almost demolished. The Germans noticed that although many monuments were evident, most in garish socialist style with flames burning in eternal fires, there were no names or unit designators to be seen on any memorial.

Arriving at the museum, perched high on the banks of the river, the party watched barges and tugs passing slowly below, laden with cargo, heading downstream toward the thirteen canals connecting the Volga to the River Don. The Russian guide continued her emotionless spiel, pointing out the various tanks, artillery pieces, and army vehicles scattered about on the museum grounds. Before the German group reached the museum, another larger group was seen approaching in the hot afternoon sun. This group was made up of men, apparently from Central Asia, wearing ornately colored skullcaps.

As the group approached the Germans it became clear that they were also veterans since most of them wore multi-colored military decorations on their left breasts. Most wore unmatched suit jackets and baggy trousers. Several were missing limbs. Their guide—an older woman—seeing the Western group, tried hard to steer her assemblage off the path that would bring the two groups together.

By this time it was obvious to the Germans that these were Red Army veterans, from Uzbekistan as it turned out, also visiting the battle scene for the first time since 1943. The veterans grew more and more curious and, as it seemed, eager to meet and converse with the former enemies. Despite frantic attempts by the two guides to prevent the groups from merging, they converged.

The apparently senior German, wearing, despite the heat, a traditional Bavarian Loden jacket with one empty sleeve neatly pinned above the elbow, stepped forward and extended his hand to the lead Uzbek, who was dressed in brown trousers, a shiny pinstripe blue jacket, and red tie, his chest bedecked with seven rows of World War II combat ribbons. The two attachés, in civilian clothing, stood aside and watched closely.

After a few minutes of urging the Germans toward the museum, the nervous guide attempted to keep the senior German from speaking with his counterpart. "Please, this is not allowed, you must follow me, separate groups are not permitted to engage in conversation."

The German ignored her and tried in vain to make himself understood to the Uzbek. Finally, the veteran turned to the West German attaché. "Please, you speak Russian, come and translate for us." The attaché stepped forward, while the guide grew visibly more upset.

"Please sir, it is forbidden, you must stop this."

The Uzbek, with whom the German was attempting to speak, turned angrily to the guide. "Hush, woman, can't you see we want to talk?"

"It's forbidden by the rules, please stop immediately."

The Uzbek swore richly in Russian, "We were good enough to fight each other; we are certainly good enough to talk together. Now leave us alone." The Russian guide blushed, burst into tears, and retired toward the museum building.

"Come," the Uzbek continued, as others from both groups pressed inward to overhear the conversation. "Where were you during all the horror?"

"I recall the tractor factory," the German replied. "See over there, we lost lots of men from my unit, a Panzer grenadier battalion. We never could dislodge you from there."

"I was near here too," replied the Uzbek veteran, pointing across the empty field, still littered with rubble from the burned-out factory. "Doesn't look the same, though, but I can feel I was near here."

"I was lucky," replied the German pointing to his empty sleeve. "I was hit somewhere near here but managed to make it to our aid station. I think, yes, probably over there in that depression." He swung his arm, pointing in the distance. "Yes, it was there, and I managed later to get to a field where I was able to get on one of the last airplanes that took the wounded out."

"Then you were not captured after the surrender?" The Uzbek looked squarely into the German's eyes.

"No, I was not, but many were and most were never seen again." He took the arm of another German. "Walther, here, was captured, and actually saw Moscow." The other German came forward.

"When did you get home?" asked the Uzbek.

"Oh, years later. But tell me, please, I don't understand why in all the places we have seen there have been no names on the monuments, no unit numbers or names."

"I don't know," responded the Uzbek after pausing to look around. He turned around and saw the Intourist guide returning with an older woman from the direction of the museum. "Here comes an expert from the museum, we'll ask her."

The crowd of veterans opened a gap for the two women to enter, the young one still showing signs of tears.

"Please, gentlemen, rejoin your groups," the older, stern-looking, stout woman said. "Germans assemble over there. Soviet citizens here. Such interaction with foreigners is prohibited for Soviet citizens."

The leading Uzbek swore loudly again. "Comrade, guide, we will do as we wish." He spat angrily on the ground showing a row of bright metal teeth. "After all, we bled here for our countries. So, now leave us in peace. Oh, but first, explain to all of us why are there no unit names and insignia of our Red Army forces displayed on the memorials. Why are the names of those who died nowhere to be found?" he asked with authority.

The woman hesitated, glancing briefly around at the veterans now pressing closer, awaiting a reply. The younger guide was again in tears.

"Names and unit numbers are still state secrets, none are to be displayed. Now cease this fraternizing with foreigners or I will call the authorities." The woman's lips began to tremble and she retreated slightly toward the museum.

The Uzbek swore at her and took the German by the arm. "Here, there are some flowers, let's go put them on the building for our comrades we lost on both sides." The attaché accompanied, translating.

The two veterans walked toward the ruined building, arm in arm, stooped to pick some wild flowers, and neared the building where they found a small plaque.

The German stopped. "What's the plaque say?

"It's to Lenin hailing the achievements of the Party in the Great Patriotic War. . . . Says nothing about the men lost here. Let's put the flowers over there. It's a perfect spot."

The two veterans stooped together, arranged the flowers, then stepped back and, still holding on to each other, saluted. They looked over the wide river, and then suddenly embraced. The others began to shake hands, some hugged, some just stared out over the river struggling with their painful memories.

Biblical Reflection

Give to the emperor the things that are the emperor's, and to God the things that are God's. Mark 12:17

The scale of the loss of life during the Battle of Stalingrad is staggering. Death and deprivation continued unchecked even after the Soviets emerged as the military victors in this battle that proved a turning point in the war on the eastern front. Of the ninety-one thousand Axis prisoners who surrendered in defeat, only slightly more than six thousand survived the harshness of long and punishing captivity.

Death on such a scale is nearly unfathomable, and yet Soviet citizens had previously experienced death on a far greater scale than Stalingrad, not as the result of military battle, but as a result of the reprehensible practices of the so-called Great Purge carried out against them by their own leaders. Intentional death came to many millions as a consequence of government policy and pogroms.

Likewise, under Nazi policies of genocide and *gleichschaltung* (synchronization), the value of human life was decided according to extreme views. *Gleichschaltung* was the process of denying human rights in favor of complete totalitarian control over individuals and society. It was considered by the Nazis to be an essential tool for achieving ideological capitulation. Under this policy of control, persons who were unwilling to bend to the dictates of the government in all aspects of their lives were considered completely expendable and could be imprisoned or killed. Despite cheerful sounding phrases such as "strength through joy" (*kraft durch freude*), complete moral capitulation to the visions of Adolf Hitler was the end goal of Nazi propaganda and policies.

Ironically, although both Stalin and Hitler embraced the notion that individuals do not matter, personality cults developed around both the Nazi and Soviet leaders. When his own son failed in a suicide attempt, Stalin is reported to have remarked, "He can't even shoot straight." Later, when speaking about national losses, he said, "A single death is a tragedy, a million deaths is a statistic."

Equally callous, Hitler, driven by racial hatred and a lust for power, wasted millions of lives. Even those in his closest inner circle came to recognize their own expendability. Hitler and Stalin, each without any compunction, directly and willfully caused the deaths of countless human beings. Men and women who might otherwise have led decent, meaningful lives became the victims of war, both those who suffered and died at the hands of others and those others who committed great wrongs against their fellow human beings at the behest of their political leaders. Though Stalin was instrumental in bringing about Hitler's downfall, his own culpability in the barbaric actions of the Soviet regime cannot be lessened simply because his nation triumphed in the Great Patriotic War.

What can one say to the survivors of both Nazi aggression and Soviet pogroms? What can be said about those who perished? What can be said of other nations that allowed such inhumane political visions to take root in neighboring countries? What can be said to the old veterans who met their former enemies at the very site of so much suffering and bloodshed? Why are the names of their fallen brothers and sisters not inscribed somewhere in recognition that they once lived?

These are not moot questions. They are questions that deserve definite answers and that have definite answers—answers that demand to be proclaimed loudly and in unmistakable and unrelenting ways until no one can claim not to have heard them, so that when the shadows of death and darkness threaten again, as they will, more people will be equipped to live according to the answers instead of suffering with just the questions.

In Germany, the Confessing Church arose in resistance and reaction to the Nazis, as Hitler's government minions attempted to take over Christian churches under the policies of *gleichschaltung* and transform them into ideological instruments. The leaders of the Confessing Church, including pastors Martin Niemoller and Dietrich Bonhoeffer, were eventually imprisoned, and in Bonhoeffer's case, hanged. They were dangerous to the Reich because of their determination to address and resist the moral wrongs of Nazi policies and aspirations.

Niemoller had, at one point, been a supporter of Nazism, but eventually he recognized the impossibility of reconciling such political beliefs with the teachings of the church. He awoke to the Nazi agenda in 1933, after Hitler established the Protestant Reich Church as the official church in Germany. The plan was for other Protestant churches to merge with this official body. Remarkably, many churches did so despite the wording of a draft called the "thirty-point program," written by Alfred Rosenberg, the architect of many of the visions Hitler espoused in his autobiographical manifesto, *Mein Kampf*.

Rosenberg's plan laid out the intentions of this so called "church." The true nature of the Protestant Reich Church became clear when the thirty-point program declared that *Mein Kampf* would replace the Bible and would be featured prominently on altars throughout Germany. (The thirty-point program was never officially adopted; however, Rosenberg had tremendous influence on German society and his ideas influenced many in the highest echelons of government.)

Unlike Hitler, who tried to co-opt religion, Stalin, who had trained at a Russian Orthodox seminary before becoming a revolutionary, forcibly suppressed religion and vehemently denied the existence of God. Each leader adopted the practice of defining humanity and of restricting human rights according to his own worldview. Hitler wanted to be God, and Stalin wanted there to be no God. Each proceeded to hold multitudes captive to their perverse visions of reality. They both forced multitudes to suffer under the seductive power of their false promises and the momentum of their political wills. They used their power to debase, not to honor, life. Decades later, war survivors still reel from the impact of such unchecked power.

These brief details of the church in Germany and of the personal practices and beliefs of the dictators provide help in answering the old veterans who met in Stalingrad years later, their sleeves empty, with the specter of oppression still uncomfortably close to them. What are the answers? Upon what did the Confessing Church base its stand against the Nazis? In short, it stood on the teachings of Jesus. In contrast to Hitler and Stalin, Jesus emphasized living in relationship with God who honors life. He understood that all human beings are created for such a relationship with God, and he knew that all human beings bear the image of the God who created them and must be treated accordingly.

Jesus taught respect for government, as is clear in his admonition to "Give to the emperor the things that are the emperor's." Yet, he insisted that we give to God alone the things that are God's. Through his quiet words, Jesus invited people then and now to think about what things must never be surrendered to another human being's control. What are these holy things of God that give ultimate meaning to life and which must never be surrendered? Scripture consistently calls for righteous behavior. Could the real meaning of human life be found in something as simple as doing what is right?

Consider some specific questions. When is it right to put living human beings in ovens? When is it right to fatally gas crowds of innocent people? When is it right to herd helpless men, women, and children toward certain death because one is "following orders"? It is *never* right to do these things. In doing such things, we align ourselves with something that is the antithesis of what God demands.

Without apology, we speak in reference to God from a Judeo-Christian point of view. The demands of God as revealed through the gospel of Jesus are radical demands. We are challenged to live firmly grounded in this life, and to understand ourselves as responsible moral beings. We are challenged to examine the moral underpinnings of all our actions.

Whether one views the world through a secular or religious lens, Jesus' teaching not to give the things that are God's to the emperor applies to all. Individuals remain responsible for their moral choices. Compromising one's own right and responsibility to make moral choices and surrendering the individual rights of anyone to satisfy governments is to give to the emperor that which belongs to God. Bad governments take root when people fail to check what the emperor demands against what God demands.

From a Christian perspective, the names of those lost at Stalingrad are inscribed in heaven, and none of the details of their lives is missing. In affirming our individual worth, Jesus taught that even the hairs of our heads are counted. So, in the matter of Jesus versus Stalin and Hitler, we find in Scripture teachings that followers of any faith or of no faith at all can access when moral choices must be made and individual fate is at question.

Again, in answer to the veterans' specific question, the names of each of the fallen are known and written; their lives mattered, to God and to those who follow God. It is certain that when old enemies meet and hug and cry together they are a beacon of hope, a sign of what's possible for those willing to recognize and respect their own humanity and the humanity of others.

CHAPTER 3

And the Blind Shall See

Along the French Norman coast, east of the Cotentin Peninsula, it is possible to visit the aging remnants of the German Atlantic Wall. These fortifications were built in the 1940s to beat back the anticipated Allied invasion of Hitler's Fortress Europe. A number of the strongest points in the wall bristled with coastal artillery pointing seaward.

Each of these strong installations has a dramatic story to tell of its eventual capture or destruction during the Allied invasion in June 1944. One of these installations is at Longues sur Mer, about midway between the famed American landing site of Omaha Beach and the British landing area called Gold Beach. When visitors today look carefully at the remaining Longues battery bunkers, they may note that two of the very sturdy concrete structures appear to be nearly destroyed while the remainder of these fortifications appear unscathed. There is a story here.

As World War II ground on in its fourth year, with the Red Army pushing slowly and painfully westward, the German High Command began to stiffen the western defenses using slave labor in anticipation of an Allied landing in France. Most of the impressed laborers came from Poland and Russia, as well as from France. The Germans built the Atlantic Wall using tens of thousands of these starving laborers. During the construction, the entire French coast was closed to local Norman farmers. The builders of the wall posted signs warning that intruders in the defensive areas would be shot.

Near the batteries of Longues sur Mer, however, the local German commander, in an unusual act of benevolence, allowed one blind French farmer to walk his neglected fields in the company of his eight-year-old grandson. The German artillerymen gazed, no doubt with dreams of home, as the two figures wandered about the fields, one using a cane and holding the boy's hand, the other guiding the old man with his young eyes.

Unknown to the German artillerymen, however, was that as the pair walked the fields, the boy was counting his paces from spot to spot, mapping out the field and accurately fixing the coastal gun positions. These measurements were carefully memorized by the old man, recorded, and later passed secretly to the local French resistance.

These invaluable measurements were sent to British intelligence in London. The invasion date was approaching and the Allied plan called for the advance destruction of as many of the coastal batteries as possible. Plans for destroying the gun emplacements included the landing of paratroopers, rangers, Royal Marine Commandos, special demolition teams, and engineers.

For Batterie Longues, however, a different scenario was in place. A Royal Navy cruiser, equipped with the exact coordinates of two of the gun emplacements, scored two direct hits in the opening salvos, completely destroying the guns inside. When elite British commandos stormed the remaining Longues batteries, the German artillerymen, stunned by the rapid loss of the two guns, surrendered without a fight. The British captured the remaining guns without suffering a single casualty. The reconnaissance work by the blind farmer and his grandson has never been publicly acknowledged.

Biblical Reflection

Samson said to the attendant who held him by the hand, "Let me feel the pillars on which the house rests, so that I may lean against them." Judges 16:26

Samson is one of the great heroes of the Bible, and even small children are familiar with the tales of his unusual strength and his remarkable ability to prevail in battle. For twenty years he was a judge in Israel. His downfall came when his Philistine wife betrayed him, and Samson became a captive of her people.

A man who had been a strong and brilliant warrior found himself robbed of his powers. Then, adding to his burdens, Samson's enemies blinded him in both eyes, imprisoned him, and bound him like an animal. He was forced to turn a wheel to grind the grain of his enemies.

Samson's enemies rejoiced at his downfall and made sport of him. They enjoyed watching his torture, and they benefited from his forced labor. In much the same way, the German High Command appropriated the labor of, abused, and harshly restricted its captives. As with Samson, however, imprisoning the body was not the same as imprisoning the mind or will or spirit of those who lived and worked under the watchful eye of their captors.

Though blinded and weakened, Samson waited and worked for the return of his physical strength, and he prayed for spiritual strength to see him through his trials. He had an inner resolve to do what he could to resist and even avenge himself on his enemies. What could a blind man do? What could an old blind man do? In either scenario, any man, blind or not, can use the gifts and strengths he has. Clearly, the ability to reason is a distinct gift of God that both Samson and the blind French farmer used.

Samson relied on the physical and spiritual strengths that had served him well in the past. When he was to be displayed for the amusement of the Philistines at a gathering, he asked a boy to lead him to the weight-bearing pillars of the hall. He planned to use what he knew about buildings to bring destruction to his enemies. With the talents that he had, Samson knew what to do to cause the roof to cave in. His blindness was no impediment to using this knowledge.

Samson's story may seem to be grossly exaggerated or embellished. Can one man make a massive building fall on thousands with just his strength, even if he is fortified by faith? Led by a young boy, one old blind man using the power of his inner vision and his ability to reason and plan brought an amazing defeat to his enemies. The enemy no doubt saw the blind old man and the young boy as being of little importance and no threat. Nevertheless, with the boy supplying the eyes to guide their way and the old man supplying the knowledge needed to map out coordinates, the two gathered invaluable information that saved many lives and defeated a formidable enemy.

Faith can inspire acts that resonate for many. No one—other than themselves and God—may have believed in the efforts of a rather helpless old man and an inconsequential little boy. But the man and the boy believed they could make a difference, and committed what abilities they had to defeating their enemies. In doing so, their power to assist the war effort was multiplied by the same power that once multiplied another little boy's loaves and fishes.

CHAPTER 4

The Meek Shall Inherit the Earth

I t is a peculiar yet pleasing phenomenon to see how, over time, the deeds of some unsung heroes eventually become widely known. This has been the case with some World War II veterans. Popular images of great battles and stirring achievements by men and women surfaced in both media and the movies during the war, a trend that continued after the dust had settled and the gore of war ended.

Many of us can probably recall Van Johnson in the movie *Thirty Seconds over Tokyo*, Burt Lancaster in *From Here to Eternity*, and John Wayne in *Sands of Iwo Jima*. As scholars and writers completed the first major research into that war's spectacular campaigns, new movies hit the screen, such as *The Longest Day* and *A Bridge Too Far*. These later stories of courage more accurately portrayed the deeds of brave men and women during the conflict.

Today a new wave of literature and film has brought heightened realism and improved accuracy to books and movies about the war. The horrors of the European war were graphically brought to life by Tom Hanks and company in Stephen Spielberg's *Saving Private Ryan*. HBO's epic *Band of Brothers* provided another well-researched look at the horrific experience of so many young soldiers. With more thorough research being done in the archives of the former enemy, new stories of unsung heroes are emerging, such as the story of William E. Ekman.

On D-Day of the Allied invasion in 1944, thirty-one-year-old Ekman, the youngest colonel in the U.S. Army, led the 505th Parachute Infantry Regiment in the capture of Sainte-Mère-Église, the first town liberated by the Allies in France. John Wayne and Red Buttons portrayed the heroic men of his regiment in the movie *The Longest Day*. Strangely, however, Ekman's name appears only briefly in the book by Cornelius Ryan from which the movie was adapted.

Ekman parachuted into Normandy with his regiment and landed astride a cow in a field in Fresville, eight kilometers northwest of his objective, Sainte-Mère-Église. He was knocked unconscious and awoke forty-five minutes later next to the cow, dead from a broken back. He was alone. Ekman removed his parachute, gathered his equipment, started toward the sound of distant firing, and promptly fell into a small canal. Barely saving himself by shedding his heavy gear, the young colonel set out again toward Sainte-Mère-Église, which he could see burning in the distance.

While crossing a field, he came across an injured medic from his regiment. The medic had broken both legs in the jump. Ekman carried him to the nearest farmhouse. The farmer's fourteen-year-old son helped carry the medic into the family's house. There the colonel and the medic set up a first aid station for the wounded.

Ekman continued to the objective, gathering stragglers from both his division and the 101st on the way. By the time the group arrived in Sainte-Mère-Église, one of his battalion commanders, Lieutenant Colonel Ben Vandervoort, and his men had secured the town and were holding more than fifty captured Germans.

In another historical classic by author Ryan, *A Bridge Too Far*, Ekman's name is again only briefly mentioned when relating the account of the Allied airborne assault during the failed attempt to capture Arnhem and break out across the Rhein into the Ruhr, the industrial heart of Nazi Germany. During that drop, the largest airborne operation in history,

Ekman's regiment captured their assigned objectives earlier than planned and fought successfully against heavy odds. Then, in December 1944, his regiment was thrown into the thick of the Battle of the Bulge. For weeks of cold combat, the 505th held its ground. Few among the surviving veterans of Ekman's own regiment know that the Belgians named a road near Bastogne "*rue du Ekman*" to commemorate his heroism and actions during the battle.

The reason behind Ekman's obscurity probably lies in the fact that he firmly believed it was not proper to sing one's own virtues, as well as his belief that he was just doing his job. Ekman was a professional with a long family military tradition. After graduating from the U.S. Military Academy (West Point) in 1933, Ekman was instrumental in forming the first units of the elite airborne forces, the newest arm of the infantry.

He initially fought as the operations officer of the 505th Parachute Infantry Regiment in North Africa. He then jumped into Sicily with the same regiment in 1943, where the regiment suffered horrendous casualties. Few today know that Ekman was already the 505th regimental commander for the D-Day assault in Normandy. He had just replaced the distinguished Brigadier General James Gavin, who jumped into Normandy as the new assistant division commander of the Eighty-second Airborne, behind Major General Mathew Ridgeway.

Ekman fought with his 505th Regiment until the war ended, at which time the regiment was assigned to patrol Berlin with the new Allied quadripartite forces in 1945. He continued his career in numerous unsung but important assignments, the most challenging of which was as the Secretary of Defense's personal representative in the 1960s. In this position he was assigned to enforce the policy of equal-opportunity housing within the armed forces.

In 1979, Brigadier General Ekman was admitted to Walter Reed Army Hospital for treatment of leukemia, probably contracted while conducting maneuvers close to atomic weapons tests in the Nevada desert in the 1950s. Once when I visited with him in the hospital, he told me the following story.

Two days after the D-Day invasion, Ekman and his troops were advancing through the town of Picauville, twelve kilometers southwest of Sainte-Mère-Église. On the outskirts of the town was a hospital staffed by sisters of a Roman Catholic order called the *Bon Savuer.* Inside the hospital grounds was a small chapel. As Ekman and his troops approached, the hospital and chapel were still burning from heavy artillery fire the day before.

During the advance, one of his troopers scrambled into the chapel for cover. The soldier spotted a large cincture rosary made with wooden beads hanging from a burning beam. He removed the rosary to keep it from igniting, stuffed it into his musette bag, left the chapel, and hurried along with his comrades. Ekman told me that he thought that someday the rosary should be returned to the hospital. He died in July 1979.

Just prior to the sixtieth D-Day commemoration ceremonies in 2004, the 505th veteran who still had the rosary, but was too ill to attend the observances, gave the rosary to William Ekman's son, Colonel Michael Ekman, airborne veteran of more recent wars. The veteran asked Ekman if he would return it for him to its original place at the *Bon Savuer* chapel.

On June 7, 2004, the mayor of Sainte-Mère-Église held a special gathering in that chapel. At a simple ceremony, Michael Ekman returned the rosary. French sisters surrounded him, the mayor, a dozen of his family members, and several 505th veterans. The rosary still hangs beside the altar, displayed on a board with a written account of its unusual odyssey.

Biblical Reflection

But when you give alms, do not let your left hand know what your right hand is doing, so that your alms may be done in secret; and your Father who sees in secret will reward you. Matthew 6:3

People who are very familiar with the Old Testament may recognize the names Bezalel and Oholiab, but generally these names are rather obscure. Like William Ekman, these two men led quietly fascinating lives. Like Ekman, they did not seek the limelight but, through their leadership and their faithfulness to their calling, they made significant contributions that benefited many others. Bezalel and Oholiab were not soldiers, but they had something in common with Ekman: their focus was not on personal recognition, but on faithfully executing their duties.

Here is their story from Exodus 35:30–36:1 NIV:

> Then Moses said to the Israelites, "See, the LORD has chosen Bezalel son of Uri, the son of Hur, of the tribe of Judah, and he has filled him with the Spirit of God, with skill, ability and knowledge, in all kinds of crafts–to make artistic designs for work in gold, silver and bronze, to cut and set stones, to work in wood and to engage in all kinds of artistic craftsmanship. And he has given both him and Oholiab son of Ahisimach, of the tribe of Dan, the ability to teach others. He has filled them with skill to do all kinds of work as craftsmen, designers, embroiderers in blue, purple and scarlet yarn and fine linen, and weavers–all of them master craftsmen and designers. So Bezalel, Oholiab and every skilled person to whom the LORD has given skill and ability to know how to carry out all the work of constructing the sanctuary are to do the work just as the LORD has commanded."

These master craftsmen, artists, and teachers were called out by name. It was their sacred duty to execute in material form the specific visions Moses had received from God. They were the ones whose hands and tools and minds were used to bring into being the tabernacle, its tent, and its covering. They, along with the men in their charge, fashioned the ark; its poles; the mercy seat; the veil of the screen; the table, lamp stand, and utensils; the altar; the court hangings; the priests' garments; and everything in which Moses had been instructed.

They saw to it that great care was taken in measuring and making the linen curtains and the goat-skin curtains down to the last detail. They worked and joined acacia wood with bases of silver to frame the tabernacle. They made bars from acacia wood and overlaid them with gold for the sides of the tabernacle. The veil of blue and purple and scarlet stuff had cherubim skillfully embroidered upon it.

Bezalel himself made the Ark of the Covenant using fine acacia wood overlaid inside and out with pure gold. He cast the rings for its corners and made the pole to go through the rings. He fashioned the mercy seat from pure gold and he made two cherubim from hammered gold, all in one piece with the mercy seat. It must have been a thing of beauty. The cherubim were executed in great detail, of hammered gold with their wings spread out above the mercy seat and their faces to one another. Imagine the care, skill, artistry, and inspiration Bezalel brought to the task of shaping these implements for the worship of God. Imagine, in fact, that each movement of Bezalel's hands and muscles along with the creative workings of his mind were themselves acts of worship as he labored to give form to vision.

Led by God and inspired to do his very best work, Bezalel formed one object after another. Likewise did Oholiab, a craftsman, designer, and embroiderer in blue and purple and scarlet, a worker with fine linen. Oholiab's work is described in intricate detail as the one who prepared the garments for

Aaron and the priests. Such fine work and creative, visionary design are by no means ordinary; rather, they result from a combination of inspiration and gifts as a craftsman.

These men worked long and hard, sparing nothing to do the work Moses commanded. They are commemorated in the book of Exodus as men who were obedient, devout, and dedicated. They are clearly men to be numbered among the world's most renowned artists. However, unlike Michelangelo or Leonardo da Vinci—artists of similar inspiration—very few today know the names Bezalel and Oholiab.

We do not know where the great artwork of Oholiab and Bezalel may be, but we know of it and can almost see it from the descriptions given to us in Scripture. What we do have from their story is the assurance that to be led in one's work is a blessing, and that great things can be performed through willing men and women whose purpose is not to have their names known, but simply to serve well and attend to their duties with dedication.

Perhaps it is God's humor and delight that in William Ekman's case, he too was instrumental—through his son—in bringing an item of beauty into a sanctuary as a matter of personal duty.

CHAPTER 5

The Golden Rule in Action

Major Gordon Smith parachuted with his men into the black night over Normandy at 1:30 A.M., June 6, 1944. His assignment, as regimental logistics officer, was to seize and occupy with his men the small village of Amfreville, six kilometers from the main Eighty-second Airborne Division objective of Sainte-Mère-Église. Smith landed in a cow pasture near Amfreville. Groping around in the hostile darkness, he gathered together several other paratroopers and set off to capture the town. They made it as far as the outskirts of the town of Gourbesville, three kilometers from Amfreville, when they ran into heavy German resistance.

With an eerie dawn breaking over the normally pastoral countryside, Smith and his men were pinned down by German machine-gun and mortar fire. Smith was hit in the left arm by a sniper. The wound was clean, but the upper arm bone was shattered. He took shelter under an apple tree and directed his men in an assault on the heavily defended town. Greatly outnumbered, the American troopers were initially repulsed.

Smith passed out under the tree from loss of blood. In a few minutes he was captured by two Germans, placed on a donkey cart, and hauled to a school in the center of Gourbesville, which had been hastily made into an aide station for the wounded.

Smith awoke some hours later to find himself in a hospital bed. A man in German uniform was perched on the foot of his bed, watching him intently. Observing the American gaining consciousness, the man in uniform hailed a doctor who quickly came to the bedside.

The doctor spoke near perfect English, but their conversation was interrupted by sounds of heavy fighting in the distance. After treating Smith's wounded arm and setting it in a temporary cast, the doctor told him, "I was captured in North Africa by the American army. I was treated well. Later I was exchanged in a prisoner of war swap for captured medical personnel. I will treat you in the same fashion that I was treated by your countrymen."

"Who is this soldier sitting on my bed, and why is he staring at me?" Smith inquired.

"That's the man who shot you. He doesn't speak German or English," the doctor explained, wiping blood from his soiled arms and hands. "He's from Byelorussia and joined us because he hates Generalissimo Joseph Stalin."

"Well, I don't care where he's from, tell him to get off my bed," Smith muttered, gaining strength from the blood plasma he had received. "He already shot me in the arm, why does he hang around me? I might just cut his throat if I can find my knife."

"Oh no, not here," the doctor replied. "We'll have no killing in this *lazarette*. There's enough killing going on outside."

Smith was transported to a German hospital in the city of Rennes, and later sent to a prisoner of war camp in Poland. In late April his camp was evacuated before the arrival of the Red Army. On May 8, following the German capitulation, he was released from custody and shipped to a convalescent hospital in Florida.

On October 15, 2006, Lieutenant Colonel Gordon Smith, with his family present, was granted honorary citizenship of the town of Gourbesville in gratitude for the sacrifices his men made in successfully liberating the town. Three hundred men from the Eighty-second Airborne Division and the Ninetieth Division lost their lives outside of Gourbesville and Amfreville.

Said Smith to the mayor of Gourbesville that day, "If it hadn't been for that German doctor, who was by the way a Christian, I wouldn't be here."

Biblical Reflection

I am the LORD, I have called you in righteousness, I have taken you by the hand and kept you; I have given you as a covenant to the people, a light to the nations, to open the eyes that are blind, to bring out the prisoners from the dungeon, from the prison those who sit in darkness. Isaiah 42:6-7

If your enemy is hungry, feed him; if he is thirsty, give him something to drink. Romans 12:20 NIV

On a mission to set French captives free from the occupying forces, Major Gordon Smith became a captive himself, but also a witness. Among his captors he encountered a doctor who encouraged him greatly. The doctor who treated Major Smith had been a prisoner himself in North Africa, and the fair and just treatment he received at the hands of his American captors resonated deep within him and influenced his treatment of Major Smith.

The doctor's American captors were, in effect, a "light to the nations." There actions mirrored Jesus' teaching in the Sermon on the Mount: "Blessed are the merciful, for they will receive mercy" (Matthew 5:7). The demonstration of just and compassionate behavior can be a catalyst for change on a scale that is impossible to measure. In freedom or in captivity, the power of light and justice can have great and wide impact.

Second Kings 5 tells the story of a captive Israelite maiden, the servant of a Syrian general's wife. The girl knew that the powerful general suffered from leprosy, and she told him of a holy man in Samaria who could cure him. General Naaman received permission from the king of Syria to see if he could find this holy man, this prophet, and be cured.

When the king of Israel received the request from the king of Syria asking him to cure the general, he was astonished and dismayed. He thought it an impossible request and simply a ruse to begin a war. But Elisha the prophet assured both the king of Israel and Naaman that his leprosy would be cured. After being persuaded to follow Elisha's simple instructions, Naaman's disease was healed; however, another pivotal, far-reaching, and unexpected change took place.

Naaman came to hold the same faith as the captive girl who had told him about the prophet in Israel who could heal him. This commander of the armies of Syria came to believe in the God of Israel. Much as it was with the German doctor, his future behavior toward others was greatly influenced by the treatment he received from Elisha. The prophet of God cured him through the power God had given him and then refused even a token of payment from the general. This touched Naaman as nothing else could have.

Righteous treatment of people has lasting effects. Opening eyes that are blind and bringing prisoners out of darkness are works of mercy. Military missions to liberate captives have the same impact as any other act of liberation. The biblical admonitions to feed the enemy if he is hungry and provide drink if he is thirsty certainly apply to war captives. Such generosity might well bring the enemy to remorse and repentance. As Romans 12:19-21 admonishes us, we are not to be overcome by evil, but to overcome evil with good. While the enemy is at our mercy, we are called to act humanely in such a way that the enemy might come to see the benefits of just and honorable behavior. The captor who is humane wins a greater victory than simply that of prevailing in battle.

It was fitting that while being honored along with the memory of the other men of the Eighty-second Airborne Division, Major Gordon Smith recalled the Christian doctor, his wartime enemy, who showed mercy to him because he had received mercy.

CHAPTER 6

Private Jake McNiece and the Dirty Dozen

Rarely does one meet a renowned character who seems totally unconcerned about his fame. Jake McNiece was raised during the Depression in a small dustbowl town in Oklahoma. Although he was known for his physical prowess and athletic ability, McNiece was by no means a model high school student and was often in trouble. When the United States found itself at war, McNiece enlisted and volunteered for the fledgling U.S. Army paratroopers "because it seemed the army's most difficult challenge."

In 1942, airborne warfare was still in its infancy and the army sought to build a growing corps of elite volunteers. Private McNiece did well in all aspects of the training, but did not care for the discipline of the regular army. He was constantly in trouble. He had joined the paratroopers to fight Germans, not to march, pick up cigarette butts, or paint rocks.

Some visionary officers who were nurturing the growth of the newest airborne division—which was to become the renowned 101st—recognized McNiece's value as a fighter and natural leader. They wisely tolerated much of his misbehavior, but still failed to keep him out of trouble. He was unable to keep stripes on his uniform. Each time he was promoted to private first class or corporal, he was soon summarily demoted for some misdeed or infraction of army regulations.

The 101st Division—the greenest U.S. airborne division—deployed to England to prepare for the Allied invasion of Hitler's Europe. While undergoing advance training for their first combat jump, McNiece's troops were bivouacked on the grounds of a wealthy English lord. Not surprisingly, the lord's precious game animals began to disappear, poached by McNiece and his hungry squad to augment their sparse wartime rations.

At this point in history, the U.S. Army had used paratroops only sparingly—once in the campaign in North Africa and then during the invasion of Sicily and Salerno, with heavy casualties. The Allied invasion plan for Normandy called for one lightly armed British and two American airborne divisions to drop behind German lines, secure strategic objectives, and hold them until the amphibious forces fought their way from the beaches. From the beginning, some senior staff officers objected to the use of the airborne, fearing excessive casualties. Nevertheless, Supreme Allied Commander General Dwight Eisenhower and Field Marshal Bernard Montgomery supported their use and overrode the objections.

For the Normandy combat jump, McNiece was assigned as temporary sergeant to lead a squad of demolition troops in the airborne division's famed 506th Parachute Infantry Regiment. Just prior to the jump, while waiting to board the troop-carrying aircraft, McNiece, who is part Choctaw Indian, shaved his head as a Mohawk. His men soon followed suit. He then smeared his face with Indian war paint and his eighteen men quickly did the same. A *Stars and Stripes* reporter caught a shot of McNiece and his men applying the war paint and shaving their heads prior to loading the planes. The photo was widely distributed in that military newspaper and eventually throughout the world. Because of their unsoldierly conduct and poor personal cleanliness while in England, the squad was called "The Filthy Thirteen." (These men and their actions in combat soon grew to legendary status and inspired the fictional movie *The Dirty Dozen*.)

Six days after heavy combat in Normandy, acting Sergeant McNiece took part in the famed bayonet charge across the flooded marshes of Carentan, driving the Germans out of that road and rail hub. While McNiece and the 506th Regiment were in the midst of the dawn assault, a frightened young French girl watched from a nearby levee. When McNiece ran by with his squad, he saw the girl, stopped, motioned her to take cover, and gave her some concentrated chocolate rations. Sixty years later during a Normandy reunion, a woman stepped out and told McNiece: "You were the American soldier who told me that day to hide. Thank you, sir, for what you and your men did for us that day." The story of their encounter was published in newspapers throughout France. It seems that, decades later, McNiece still could not avoid publicity.

Carentan was taken by the 101st paratroopers on June 12,1944, after which the troops enjoyed a brief respite. After three days of cleaning out the remaining Germans in the town, McNiece's squad was resting and recouping in the town center. They suddenly received intense close-range sniper fire. McNiece quickly noticed that the fire was coming from high in the Carentan cathedral. Reacting immediately, he took squadmate Jack Womer and ran to the cathedral.

A priest blocked the entrance, saying, "This is sacred ground; there will be no fighting in my church."

Without hesitating McNiece responded, "Move aside Father, there are snipers in your steeple. If you don't stand aside we'll shoot you first and then go after 'em."

The priest wisely moved aside. McNiece and Womer scrambled up the stone stairs toward the steeple, immediately taking fire from above. McNiece lobbed a grenade up the stairs and advanced through the smoke. He found two French men and one woman, apparently ready to die rather than face their townspeople as collaborators. McNiece and Womer killed them and tossed their bodies from the steeple into the churchyard below. Later, they were thanked by the local inhabitants, who confirmed the three dead were notorious collaborators.

On June 22, General Maxwell Taylor, 101st Division commander, held a brief award ceremony in the center of Carentan. While he was giving out combat decorations, a German 88 artillery piece opened fire from about eight miles away. The pre-registered rounds landed with great accuracy in the town center, killing seven American troops and decapitating a young French girl who was handing flowers to the Americans in the ceremony. She died in the arms of one of McNiece's men.

After thirty-six days of intense combat in Normandy, the 101st was withdrawn to England to prepare for its next parachute assault. The unit had lost more than sixty percent of its men. In September of the same year, they jumped again, this time into Holland as part of operation Market Garden, designed to seize and hold the town of Arnhem and cross the Rhein River into Germany.

After that mission McNiece returned to England and volunteered to be a Pathfinder, a soldier who parachuted ahead of the main force to mark the drop zones. The story of McNiece's Pathfinders during the Battle of the Bulge has yet to be recorded in the many accounts of that battle.

On December 16, 1944, after the Germans launched their last-ditch offensive in the Ardennes, the 101st Airborne Division, then refitting in France, was sent by truck with the Eighty-second Airborne Division to plug the gap caused by the retreating American forces. McNiece and his Pathfinders were still in England, training with new radio-homing equipment for future operations.

After days of intense combat his division was surrounded in the freezing woods of Bastogne. Heavy ground fog and snow prevented both resupply and much-needed air support. In a desperate attempt to help them, McNiece's Pathfinders were marshaled to drop between the lines to mark a resupply mission with their new radio beacons. On the day before Christmas Eve, McNiece's two squads left England on what appeared to be a suicide mission. Despite the heavy overcast and thick ground fog, the gifted pilots dropped McNiece and his men from two low-flying C-47 Skytrain troop carriers.

McNiece and his twenty-two men landed precisely between the German and American lines, with the famed 506th regiment providing cover fire with dwindling ammunition. According to McNiece, he and his men landed near a cemetery and raced for shelter amid the gravestones. He and his team set up homing beacons and directed in more than seven hundred airplanes that dropped much needed relief goods—food, ammunition, medical supplies, and winter clothing—through the thick overcast. Although some of the resupply material fell into German hands, the mission provided sufficient supplies for the embattled 101st paratroopers to hold out until the skies cleared on December 26, when tactical air cover and additional relief supplies were able to reach the beleaguered division.

For some reason, historians have overlooked this successful Pathfinder mission. McNiece and his men survived and jumped again in Prueme, Germany, in 1945, to support the crossing of the Rhein River. They fought on until the last days of German resistance, finally capturing Hitler's alpine redoubt at Berchtesgarden, Bavaria.

After the war McNiece returned to Oklahoma and took a job as a postman. In his eighties at this writing, McNiece is not a religious man, but he spends his time speaking to young children, imparting the strengths of American values and leadership. His thrilling, still mostly untold stories are enough to render awe in any man, woman, or child.

Biblical Reflection

The king of Egypt said to the Hebrew midwives, one of whom was named Shiphrah and the other Puah, "When you act as midwives to the Hebrew women, and see them on the birthstool, if it is a boy, kill him; but if it is a girl, she shall live." But the midwives feared God; they did not do as the king of Egypt commanded them, but they let the boys live. Exodus 1:15-17

Exceptionally brave people come in a variety of guises. Exodus 1:15-22 describes two very defiant people whom many of us would be hard pressed to name but who match this description.

They worked together as midwives, providing a very needed service in their community. They were Hebrew slaves and yet they resisted even Pharaoh when it came to doing what they knew to be right. Shiphrah and Puah are their names. In most ways these women led typical lives, serving in an appreciated but unremarkable capacity.

What made them heroic? When Pharaoh demanded that all male Hebrew infants be killed at birth, they devised ways to save the infants and concocted stories to thwart Pharaoh's attempts to destroy the male children, in spite of the danger to themselves. Clearly, they could have been killed if discovered. They acted in defiance anyway.

Jake McNiece was not a poster boy for military bearing, yet, like Shiphrah and Puah—and also like Samson—he consistently performed with bravery despite his sometimes unconventional methods. McNiece was an American soldier, expected to serve in a disciplined, orderly, and obedient manner. Samson was a judge of Israel, set apart as a Nazirite, and dedicated to God, and yet Samson hardly fit the expected model of a holy man. He loved a good brawl, loved to drink, loved to bet and carouse, had a legendary temper, and had an appetite for women that chronically got him into situations quite at odds with pious living.

Was Samson heroic? He was not concerned about appearances but about results. Like any other person, Samson was in no way perfect, but he got the job done. Even when he faltered, Samson managed to keep his goals in mind. Despite his problems with profligacy, Samson maintained a basic reliance on God as part of his arsenal of personal weapons, and approached God through prayer. As the story is told, Samson suffered greatly as a result of his own very poor choices, but God still answered Samson's prayers.

It was Jesus who taught by example how to recognize the potential hero in unexpected places and people. It was Jesus who mingled with the crowds, ate with tax collectors, kept company with rough fishermen, conversed with women whom others scorned, welcomed little children, shared fellowship with the poor and the rich, the weak and the powerful, the learned and the unlearned. When ordinary people like Matthew, Peter, Saul, and the unnamed woman at the well came into Jesus' presence, they found themselves strangely transformed into people capable of far more than they thought they were capable of. Like the military commanders who looked beyond what McNiece did not do to what he could do, Jesus saw (and sees) what people can do and can become.

It might embarrass McNiece to be compared to someone like Peter, whom the world considers a saint, but Peter might very much enjoy being compared to Jake McNiece in his humanity and readiness to answer the call to serve and assist others.

CHAPTER 7

Father Forgive Them

I couldn't sleep on the Boston-to-Frankfurt flight. Despite the dimmed cabin lights, I remained awake and found myself in deep conversation with a couple returning to Germany from stateside business. The woman, named Iris, slim, handsome, and middle-aged, was born in Dresden in the 1950s. She and her husband lived near that ancient city with their two teenaged children.

After several hours of conversation, I learned that her father's first wife and child had died in the terrible bombing of Dresden in March 1945, while her father, a Wehrmacht officer, was a prisoner of war in the Soviet Union. He was released in 1952, and returned to his native Dresden only to learn his wife and daughter were gone.

Iris spoke of the reconstruction of the city, more than eighty percent destroyed by the back-to-back Allied raids. The bombing attacks were particularly devastating since the Gothic city, until then untouched by the war, was filled with tens of thousands of refugees fleeing the Red Army. The Royal Air Force bombers struck at night causing massive damage and casualties. The British attack was followed by an armada of nearly eight hundred U.S. Air Force bombers, which struck early the next morning as the city's inhabitants and refugees were emerging from their shelters. Casualty figures vary according to the source, but it may have been in excess of eighty thousand, mostly civilians.

Popular German accounts claim there were no military targets in the city to warrant such a devastating strike. Today, however, documented archives have confirmed that the Germans had hastily moved much of their armament industry, displaced from the east, into Dresden to avoid its capture by the Red Army. The Allies planned the raids specifically to prepare for the Soviet assault in the spring of 1945, which opened the final Russian pincer drive to Berlin.

After telling of the return of her father to what remained of the once beautiful city, birthplace of composers, writers, and artists, on the banks of the sweeping River Elbe, Iris explained that the cathedral in the center of Dresden had been destroyed in the air raid. The East German regime disappeared in 1997, after leaving the cathedral in ruins as a monument to the war for more than forty-five years. With the end of East Germany, reconstruction of the cathedral began with the hope that it would be reconsecrated in 2004.

Iris showed me her wristwatch. On the face of the watch I could see the outline of the cathedral. A blackened outline showed the remaining ruins and a gold outline depicted the planned reconstruction. Embedded in the face of the watch was a small piece of original stone from the cathedral. The watches were being sold to help raise funds for rebuilding.

About two hours out of Frankfurt, I began to explain to Iris that a good friend of mine from Kennebunk, Maine, Charles Alling, had led the March 1945 raid on Dresden. Chuck had been a twenty-six-year-old command pilot of an Air Force B-17 Flying Fortress based in England. During the approach for the early morning raid, the group commander's lead aircraft was hit and destroyed by German anti-aircraft fire. Automatically—and according to the operation order—Chuck's airplane filled the slot and led the formation in the attack.

Chuck Alling is an unusual man. Following the war he returned to studies at Yale University, graduated, and became a successful businessman in Manhattan. He organized an ethics-in-business group in New York City and, following retirement, still heads the ethics-in-business movement in the state of Maine. Chuck lectures and is a leader in the Episcopal Church of Saint David's in Kennebunk. He has been active in the church as a vestry member, lay reader, and chalice bearer.

As I talked about Chuck's experience and character, I noticed Iris had grown silent. After a long pause, she removed her wristwatch, and with tears coursing down her cheeks said, "Here, give this to Mr. Alling on my behalf." When we landed in Frankfurt I bade farewell to Iris and her husband, assuring her that I would give the watch to my friend.

Later that year, in the garden of Saint David's, with the Bishop of Maine present, I told the story and presented the watch to Chuck. He accepted the watch in silence, but was obviously deeply moved. Later I learned that he had initiated a regular correspondence with Iris and had become a major financial contributor to the rebuilding of the cathedral.

I visited Dresden in June 2004, just following the cathedral's reconsecration. As I stood in silence contemplating the cathedral and comparing it with the ruins I had seen in 1986 while touring the German Democratic Republic, I noticed a man standing near me taking detailed pictures with a collection of elaborate cameras. In the resulting conversation, I learned from the man, who said he was an engineer, that the cathedral had not been hit during the bombing raid at all. Rather, sparks and flames from adjacent burning buildings had ignited the ancient cathedral's wooden roof, leading to its destruction.

I took that bit of information back home to Chuck and told him that he had not really hit the cathedral. He then told me that following the war he made a visit to Coventry Cathedral in England, which had been demolished in a German bombing raid much earlier in the war. Chuck described how, to visit the new cathedral, one had to walk through the burned-out old chancel where the original altar still stood. On the altar stood a cross, made of burnt wood from the destroyed church. Etched in glass above the entrance to the new nave were the words, "Father Forgive Them," in both German and English.

Biblical Reflection

Why should my face not be sad, when the city, the place of my ancestors' graves, lies waste, and its gates have been destroyed by fire? Nehemiah 2:3b

In the book of Nehemiah, the prophet provides an autobiographical account of his attempts, following the Babylonian Captivity, to restore Jerusalem (destroyed by Nebuchadnezzar's army in 586 B.C.). Although it was many years later—around 444 B.C.—that Nehemiah led a wave of returning Jews to Jerusalem, he was determined to rebuild the city's defenses, restore the city's former glory, and reinvigorate the culture that had been kept alive in the collective memory of former captives.

Nehemiah was inspired to act decisively after he received accounts of the extent of the ruins in Jerusalem from his brother Hanani, who had personally seen the damage. Based on Hanani's report, Nehemiah sought both permission and materials from King Artaxerxes to begin work on a restoration project. He asked for letters of safe passage, for timbers, and for army officers to assist him. The king granted his requests.

Upon reaching Jerusalem, Nehemiah took a few men and inspected the extent of the ruins for himself. He performed his survey secretly at night, aware that the enemies of Jerusalem still had power to interfere with his plans. Nevertheless, following his inspection, he organized workers who committed themselves to repairing the broken-down walls of Jerusalem and rebuilding the city gates, which had been burned.

The restoration was not a welcome development to everyone living in the area and the work was met with great resistance. In fact, guards had to be posted on the walls, and Nehemiah wrote about his workmen that, "the burden bearers carried their loads in such a way that each labored on the work with one hand and with the other held a weapon. And each of the builders had his sword strapped at his side while he built" (Nehemiah 4:17-18).

Despite opposition, the wall was completed in a record fifty-two days, a testament to vision and purpose. Much more than a symbol, the wall was a concrete source of inspiration to returning captives, pointing to other things they might realistically hope would be restored in their lives.

Nehemiah, though a devout holy man, began with the infrastructure, the hard work of supplying the means for physical security and shelter. It was only after the reconstruction that Nehemiah turned his attention to fully reminding his people of the strengths of their faith and the beliefs that had seen them through the bitterness of captivity, though that faith had been the impetus behind the rebuilding. The real restoration was still to come.

In both stories, "Father Forgive Them" and the story of Nehemiah, the workers had their swords close at hand while rebuilding. The weapons that guard the mind and spirit from despair, as well as the physical weapons that guard the body, were essential in restoration. Hope and vision were equal to the wood, stones, and mortar in bringing about a sense of meaningful restoration.

CHAPTER 8

The Return

As mentioned in "The Battle of Pilar Pass," my father was a U.S. Army chaplain, and he influenced me a great deal in my younger years. In 1954, he was assigned to Germany as the Southern Area command chaplain in charge of arranging divine services for all U.S. troops in southern Germany. One of his most time-consuming tasks was ensuring that chaplains of all faiths were available along the iron curtain borders, primarily the Czechoslovakian and East German borders, where American armored reconnaissance troops patrolled daily.

Dad's work may have seemed dull compared to the hair-raising Cold War confrontations in Berlin, where the four-power Allies mixed daily, cheek-by-jowl, with Soviet and East German forces. For a fifteen-year-old, however, my father's work was exciting.

I often traveled with my father, usually by car or jeep, along the stark iron curtain borders while he arranged Sunday services for the front-line troops. I was enthralled, watching the Czech guards patrolling with dogs along the border and reading the signs warning of mine fields. At first it seemed strange to me that the communist border guards always faced inward, rather than outward. I soon realized, however, that their main function was to prevent their own citizens from leaving the country.

One Sunday in June 1955, my father and I boarded the train in Hof, leaving the border area for Munich. I always enjoyed traditional European train compartments where passengers sat eight to a compartment off a long passageway running the length of the car. After boarding the train, we entered a compartment that held two other passengers, women headed for small towns between Hof and Munich.

Just before the train pulled out of the station, a middle-aged man entered our compartment. He seemed very shy, and he carried one suitcase made of cardboard that was obviously brand new. He smiled at the four occupants and then, after carefully thrusting his suitcase onto the rack above, settled into a seat. I recall thinking that he seemed a very meek but nice man. He was wearing a shiny new suit, and wore leather sandals, the type often seen in the East. His hair was cropped short, and he had pink marks along his neck from shaving.

The train rattled on for the three-hour trip to Munich. My father, seizing the opportunity to practice his German, struck up a conversation with the man. He said his name was Walther and he was returning from Russia as a newly released prisoner of war. My father questioned him, enjoying Walther's unraveling saga.

Walther had been captured in 1942, after his armored reconnaissance patrol had penetrated Moscow. He had driven his recon vehicle down Gorky Street late at night and had the Kremlin in view, not one thousand meters away, when Soviet military police sighted the vehicle and forced it to retreat toward Khimki, the point of deepest penetration by the Germans into Moscow. Walther was captured when his vehicle overturned after skidding near the Aeroport Metro station on Leninskiy Shausse.

My father and Walther kept talking while I tried my best to keep up. At one point I noticed the conductor approaching to check tickets. He punched our tickets in routine fashion, and then Walther handed him a letter. He read it, and then stiffened and saluted while saying, "It's an honor to have you on our train."

This exchange piqued my father's curiosity and he asked Walther where he was going. He said he was returning to Traunstein, his home before leaving for war in 1942. My father immediately felt the immensity of this journey for Walther. "Does anyone know you are retuning?" he asked.

"Well, I'm not sure," Walther replied. "My sister, Christa, told me on the telephone before I left Hof that she would be there when I arrive."

"Do you have other family?" my father asked.

"Not sure," Walter responded. "I did, but I'm afraid they may be gone, since I've heard nothing in ten years."

My father retreated into one of his frequent "before-the-sermon" quiet periods. Then, as the train approached Traunstein, Walther pulled his suitcase down, said goodbye to my father, and walked slowly to the end of the coach. As the train pulled in to the station, we suddenly heard the music of a brass band. Scores of people were on the platform carrying a banner saying, "Welcome home Wally."

I rarely saw my father moved, but that day he cried.

Biblical Reflection

For it is the God who said, "Let light shine out of darkness," who has shone in our hearts to give the light of the knowledge of the glory of God in the face of Jesus Christ. 2 Corinthians 4:6

One of the treasures in my house is a small worn volume of the New Testament. The brown leather cover is cracked, and the lettering on it is barely legible. It was presented to my husband in 1972, with the inscription, "2 Corinthians 4:6." Corrie ten Boom, the respected evangelist, signed her name with a flourish when she presented the gift to him. The blue ink has paled, but the top of the "C" in her name has the appearance of a heart. I don't know if this is whimsical fancy on my part or an intentionally inscribed motif, but the little flourish stands as a personal connection to this woman who was such a hero of the faith.

Corrie ten Boom's story has something to say to Walther's story in "The Return." Her family suffered greatly under the Nazi regime in whose army Walther served. Though her story is one of ultimate spiritual triumph, it is also a story of horrendous imprisonment, persecution, and great loss when she and her family were betrayed for helping Jews attempting to escape the Holocaust.

After immense suffering and deprivation in Nazi concentration camps, and after losing her sister Betsie and her father in the death camps, Ten Boom was set free. She spent the remainder of her life as an evangelist proclaiming her faith in Christ and inviting others to share that faith, but there was a time when that faith was severely tested.

In 1947, she appeared in a church in Munich to speak about forgiveness. She spoke about her and Betsie's experience in Ravensbruck, a notorious and inhumane camp where Betsie died from mistreatment. Ten Boom spoke eloquently about forgiveness, and then she saw him: a man clutching a brown hat approaching her with great purpose. In her mind's eye the hat was transformed into a hated uniform cap.

As the man neared, Ten Boom felt again the horrors of her captivity. She recognized this man as one of the guards at Ravensbruck. When he reached her, he told Ten Boom that he had become a Christian and he begged her forgiveness. Finally he stretched out his hand to her, waiting.

Did she take his hand? Could she take his hand? A similar question could be asked of anyone reading Walther's story. Can we join Walther's homecoming celebration? I don't know Walther's entire story. I do know he fought for the Germans and that he was captured and imprisoned by the Soviets. I know I am glad the Germans were defeated. I know I am sorry for the cruel treatment of German prisoners by the Soviets. Still, what do I have to know about Walther to join in the tears that were shed at his homecoming? In light of what

I know about the suffering imposed on millions due to the war machinery of Germany, is it right for me to be moved by Walther's plight?

Ten Boom's faith was severely tested when she was asked to forgive a man who had terribly persecuted her and been instrumental in the death of her beloved sister. In her own words:

And I stood there—I whose sins had every day to be forgiven—and could not. Betsie had died in that place—could he erase her slow terrible death simply for the asking? It could not have been many seconds that he stood there, hand held out, but to me it seemed hours as I wrestled with the most difficult thing I had ever had to do.

For I had to do it—I knew that. The message that God forgives has a prior condition: that we forgive those who have injured us. "If you do not forgive men their trespasses," Jesus says, "neither will your Father in heaven forgive your trespasses..."

And still I stood there with the coldness clutching my heart. But forgiveness is not an emotion—I knew that too. Forgiveness is an act of the will, and the will can function regardless of the temperature of the heart. "Jesus, help me!" I prayed silently. "I can lift my hand, I can do that much. You supply the feeling."

And so woodenly, mechanically, I thrust my hand into the one stretched out to me. And as I did, an incredible thing took place. The current started in my shoulder, raced down my arm, sprang into our joined hands. And then this healing warmth seemed to flood my whole being, bringing tears to my eyes.

"I forgive you, brother!" I cried. "With all my heart!"

For a long moment we grasped each other's hands, the former guard and the former prisoner. I had never known God's love so intensely as I did then.[1]

No one can speak as eloquently or as meaningfully as one who has been there. Ten Boom emerged from the abyss to inscribe Bibles with verses about the penetrating power of light, and able to write books about forgiving the most grievous trespasses.

Walther had been a perpetrator of war, a victim of war, and a prisoner of war. A town turned out to celebrate his return when so many others of his generation were lost forever. Who was Walther that anyone should weep and be glad at his return, that a brass band should play and banners wave? I don't know. I only know that, following Ten Boom's example, I can will myself to stretch my faith and my imagination in an act of affirmation toward a fellow human being. In reading this story, I can call up compassion and figuratively stretch out my own hand and wait for God to supply the current of healing energies that cauterize even the wounds of war and burn away every image for me, except the image of God in a man.

Forgiveness. It is not for me to forgive the particular trespasses of another that were committed against someone else. That would be an empty gesture on my part, even a mockery in some sense. If my sister wasn't killed, my father brutalized, and my future obscured, then words of forgiveness cannot and should not come from me. As the outsider hearing the stories, I can learn from the example of others and examine my own moral responses in the wake of their tragedies and in the light of the Word. I can make a conscious decision about how I will believe and how I will proceed.

CHAPTER 9

In God We Trust

I first met Colonel Freeman Bruce Olmstead at the military attaché training course in Washington, D.C. He and his wife Gail were heading to Copenhagen, I to Belgrade. We soon became close friends and shared many good times while attending the grueling language training at the Foreign Service Institute.

Most of our classmates were recent college graduates, average age of twenty-two, and heading for their first posting abroad in the foreign service. For those of us who were middle-aged and had already served twenty years driving airplanes and ships, it was a challenging experience, to put it mildly, to suddenly sit in language lessons, six hours a day, five days a week.

Bruce was always positive, and despite the linguistic hurdles, learned the Danish language with flair. Bruce had suffered more than most men our age, in extraordinary situations, yet he didn't show it. While I wouldn't describe Bruce as religious, I certainly knew he was a believer and held strong values of Christian ethics.

Bruce was an air force combat pilot with twenty years of flying experience. On July 1, 1960, he was flying a six-engine reconnaissance plane on a routine electronic surveillance mission over the Barents Sea off the northern coast of the U.S.S.R. When he was about 130 miles north of the Kola Peninsula, a Soviet MiG-19 fighter piloted by Lieutenant Vasili Poliakov shot down his aircraft. Bruce survived the crash, and awoke in his life raft with a broken back.

He fought for hours in the near freezing temperature to stay awake and, despite the pain, tried to find a rescue ship in the vicinity. At one point, after hours of struggle and in deep despair, he took out his pistol and prepared to end the torment of slowly freezing to death. But he couldn't give up; he threw the pistol into the sea and kept on trying to survive. Eventually he passed out and awoke hours later aboard a Russian fishing trawler, being fed a cup of brandy-laced tea by burly Russian fishermen.

Bruce and the only other survivor—the navigator—were sent to Moscow's Lubyanka prison. There, Bruce was given rudimentary medical care. The Russian doctors treated his broken back by tying him in a metal-frame prison bed with weights for traction. He slowly healed while losing more than eighty pounds.

President John F. Kennedy, in the initial months of his presidency, refused to talk with or meet the Soviet ambassador to Washington until the two airmen were released from prison. The Cold War was at its coldest. During that period, 350 U.S. airmen from both the navy and the air force were shot down and killed by the Soviets during reconnaissance missions over international waters. After eleven torturous months, Bruce and the navigator were released in a prisoner exchange for the captured Soviet spy Colonel Abel.

Bruce served for three years in Copenhagen as U.S. air and defense attaché and then retired to Annapolis, Maryland, to enjoy the sailing and model building he loved. In retirement, however, Bruce nurtured a strange yearning to visit the new Russia, shed of its failed communist system. Finally, in 1996, at the invitation of some former Soviet officers, Bruce visited St. Petersburg.

The Russians knew of Bruce's ordeal and incarceration as it had been covered in the Russian press. Several newspapers interviewed Bruce and filmed a documentary about his ordeal for Russian national television. Bruce even spoke once with Vasili Poliakov, the man who had shot him down. Afterward he said he was happy at last to have overcome his hostility over the loss of his four other crewmen.

Bruce's strong character was to be tested again. In 2005, Bruce and Gail lost their youngest daughter to suicide. A year later, I had a chance to meet with Bruce, and I expected him to still be shattered by the loss. I found, however, that despite his grief, the same inner strength that kept him alive in that life raft, tossing on the freezing Barents Sea more than forty years earlier, had enabled him to remain a strong and vibrant person.

Biblical Reflection

Rather, as servants of God we commend ourselves in every way: in great endurance; in troubles, hardships and distresses; in beatings, imprisonments and riots; in hard work, sleepless nights and hunger; in purity, understanding, patience and kindness; in the Holy Spirit and in sincere love; in truthful speech and in the power of God; with weapons of righteousness in the right hand and in the left; through glory and dishonor, bad report and good report; genuine, yet regarded as imposters; known, yet regarded as unknown; dying, and yet we live on; beaten, and yet not killed; sorrowful, yet always rejoicing; poor, yet making many rich; having nothing, and yet possessing of everything. 2 Corinthians 6:4-10 NIV

There are similarities in Bruce Olmstead's experiences and the experiences of Paul of Tarsus. The apostle Paul was imprisoned many times during the course of his evangelistic efforts. Once during a visit to Philippi he was attacked by a crowd, had his clothes torn off by the magistrates, and was then severely beaten before being shackled in an inner prison cell and left to suffer.

In reading the story of someone so far removed from us in time, it is easy to divorce ourselves from the reality of the physical pain and brutality he suffered. We can understand with a more intimate level of compassion the suffering of contemporaries. We can imagine what it must have been like to crash into the sea, suffer a broken back, nearly freeze to death, and then endure the rigors of imprisonment by hostile forces while on starvation rations. Nevertheless, in each case, real men suffered and lived through crucibles of real pain, the scope of which only they could truly understand.

The suffering of men like Paul and Bruce counts. They suffered in the course of attempting to bring opportunity to others to live life at its fullest. Their seemingly dissimilar missions had very similar goals and required very similar levels of commitment. Some might be offended at the comparison, but recall the faith of the centurion, whom Jesus praised; recall the faith of military men like David and Joshua. Can we not say that the protectors of our rights and bodies are as much servants of God as those who lead us in our spirituality? And do not those who lead us in our spirituality also often face surprising dangers as they commit to the journeys necessary to bring the Word to others?

Bruce Olmstead and Paul of Tarsus drew from the same source as they performed their duties. The compulsion to keep going when under great duress, the choice to do the right thing when other alternatives were available, and the decision to remain faithful to their callings reveal inner resources grounded on shared principles of service to others.

St. Paul was vocal in proclaiming the ultimate source of his strength. His primary mission was to make known to the world the person and cause of Christ. Paul wrote in Ephesians 4:1, "As a prisoner for the Lord, then, I urge you to live a life worthy of the calling you have received. Be completely humble and gentle; be patient, bearing with one another in love. Make every effort to keep the unity of the Spirit through the bond of peace" (NIV).

Bruce had the benefit of anchoring his ethics in Christian teaching based in large part on Paul's writings. His role as a military man can easily be compared to the roles of others in Scripture, and guarding the bonds of peace can rightly be viewed as his calling.

In the Old Testament we read that Joshua sent out a reconnaissance team before he went on the march to take Jericho. King David frequently sent men ahead to gather information so that his decisions and strategies might be the best ones possible. Without the willingness of such risk takers to go and see what potential enemies might be planning, those who work for justice and safety would be severely limited in their efforts. The prophet Micah declared, "He has showed you, O man, what is good. And what does the Lord require of you? To act justly and to love mercy and to walk humbly with your God" (Micah 6:8 NIV).

The Bruces of the world, in enabling and protecting possibilities for justice and mercy, allow the Pauls of the world to proclaim divine words that lead to paths of justice and mercy. The work and sufferings of such servants serve to commend them in every way.

CHAPTER 10

Never Walk Alone

D uring the period following the 1968 communist Tet offensive in Vietnam, the U.S. Mekong patrol forces frequently sent out boat patrols carrying a volunteer doctor and nurse with medical supplies to treat the inhabitants of villages located deep in communist-controlled areas. These patrols were called MEDCAPs. Their objectives were to minister to the villagers' minor ailments and to transport seriously sick people to South Vietnamese-controlled towns for treatment. The humanitarian mission was critical because travel during those months for the ordinary citizen was totally cut off and no other help was available.

One hot and humid afternoon in February 1968, I led a three-boat MEDCAP patrol carrying an Australian doctor and nurse and a small team of Vietnamese regional infantry to an isolated village located deep inside a canal running between two towns on the upper Mekong in Sa Dec Province. We had not visited the village since the offensive began three weeks earlier, and the area was reported as tightly controlled by the Viet Cong. We had alerted the U.S. Army Ninth Division headquarters, fifty miles down river, regarding our operation in case we needed helicopter gunship support.

After an uneventful but tense excursion some fifteen miles down a narrow canal, we arrived at the small village. Already a gaggle of children and curious villagers had gathered on the canal's bank. It was our practice to never announce our visits in advance. If we had, the enemy would ambush us within the narrow canals where our fast but unarmored fiberglass thirty-one-foot boats were most vulnerable.

We beached the boats bow on to the shore, sent out the perimeter security force, and unloaded the medical team. I ordered the security team, made up of American volunteer sailors and Vietnamese regional troops, to create a thin line for forward observation and early warning about fifty yards around the outer village perimeter. By the time the team had set up, scores of local villagers had assembled around the boats.

The medical team began their tedious routine. Having been warned by the local South Vietnamese Army district command about recent sightings of several battalions of the enemy, I walked out from the river bank accompanied by my Vietnamese sidekick, a very shell-shocked sergeant of the South Vietnamese river police. Sergeant Dinh had been in the South Vietnamese Rangers and, over the years, had been wounded severely several times in combat. He was highly nervous and claimed to be able to smell the enemy. In this case he proved correct.

For the entire morning the medical team treated the villagers, from pregnant women to ill and injured children and the aged. After a short break for lunch they continued their ministrations until late afternoon. On the outskirts of town, I sent Sergeant Dinh back to check on the number of villagers still waiting in line for treatment. Just as he left, I heard several distant bursts of automatic fire beyond a tree line several hundred yards away from the canal. I circled quickly looking for our security troops and to my chagrin could find none. I looked further and heard more sporadic fire. I spotted three of our security men running back toward the village.

As I looked around, it became quickly evident that I was quite alone. Suddenly a series of explosions landed near a cluster of straw huts, mortar fire too distant to be a direct threat. I continued to circle looking for more of our regional troops when I heard a blood-curdling wail coming from the direction of the huts where the mortar rounds had landed. I approached slowly. The tormented sounds seemed like those of a young woman. Still seeing no others and hearing the shooting grow fainter and finally stop, I followed the sound of whimpering and crying. Inside one hut I found a young girl bleeding from a shrapnel wound in the back. I approached slowly and saw she was still conscious but bleeding heavily. An elderly Vietnamese woman was cradling her and wailing like a banshee. The hut smelled like fish sauce, charcoal smoke, and blood.

I tried to calm the woman and gently helped to stop the girl's blood flow by tying over the wound a bandage from my battle dressing kit. After the woman stopped wailing it grew quiet. The young girl did not cry, although she was still conscious. It was late afternoon and the shadows were lengthening. Fearing the girl might bleed to death, I decided to carry her to the boats. Out in the open of the village, with the woman trailing behind me, it was eerily silent. No one was in sight. This stillness and absence of people were usually warnings that the villagers expected battle. Villagers were, in my experience, usually correct, and they voted with their feet, leaving all their belongings in place. I was carrying only a side arm, a regulation Colt 45 in a leather holster, and now the young girl, although not heavy, rendered my progress awkward.

After covering about fifty yards toward the canal, I noticed the woman behind me had suddenly bolted for a tree line. Growing concerned, I had to shift the girl. I laid her down and tried adjusting the dressing on her wound. When I looked up I found myself staring into the face of a man less than twenty yards away. I froze, maintaining eye contact. He too seemed to freeze, looking straight into my eyes.

He looked to be in his middle years, although estimating Vietnamese ages is not a skill easily mastered. I noticed he had short hair, graying slightly. He had intelligent black eyes and a typical Vietnamese male face marked with several nasty scars. He appeared to be unarmed, and wore a blue sort of jumpsuit.

I remained still as he approached. He stopped in front of me and looked closely at the girl. In my rudimentary Vietnamese I told him I was taking her to the boats and a medical team. He looked closely at me and questioned, using his hands and fingers, some of which, I noticed, were mere stumps.

He seemed to be asking, "How many boats and men?" I shrugged, not about to answer. Let him guess, I thought. Might be a good tactic in case he was an enemy.

The two of us and the girl remained the only people visible in the clearing. Sensing that I was growing tense, the man put his hand on my arm. He pointed to my pistol and shook his head implying no, then he put his fingers to his lips signaling silence. He helped me pick up the girl and motioned me ahead. Together we carried the limp girl toward the canal bank where the boats were, about five hundred yards ahead.

We walked slowly and I saw that he was shod only in sandals, his feet hardened and gnarled. The unwavering gaze of his intense black eyes gave me the sense of an unusual commanding presence. Just before reaching the clearing, where the boats were, I heard a loud voice hailing me. "Lieutenant sir, come back, sir, we got to haul it quick."

The man signaled me to stop, looking alert but not frightened. He looked around, quickly sizing up the situation. Then he helped me take the girl alone, adjusting her onto my back. He turned and looked square into my eyes. He put his hands together in the Vietnamese form of showing respect, nodded briefly, and then quickly darted into the village where he disappeared. Before he vanished I noticed the bulge of a pistol tucked in the back of his coveralls.

I began to walk quickly toward the boats, and after covering a few yards I saw three of my sailors, helmet-clad, wearing flak jackets, carrying M-16 rifles, running toward me in a semi-arc, then falling to the ground in firing position. Petty Officer Queenan, my senior boat captain, ran forward, grabbed the girl from me, and pushed me forward as we ran together across the field.

"Sir, we just got the word from ARVN [South Vietnamese] headquarters, a conference of senior VC from a couple battalions is taking place near here."

"Where's the team?" I asked as we ran.

"I sent them in the first boat heading toward the main river." Then he asked where I had been.

"Never mind, I'm here now. Any other news?"

"Yes sir, in a few minutes the ARVN Ninth Division is going to put in a barrage right about fifty meters from where you were; that's supposedly where the meeting is taking place right now."

We reached the last of the three boats, bow beached on the bank, engines running. The gunners, stern but cool, were manning their fifty-caliber guns. Eager hands took the girl from Queenan. I jumped in the boat, the engines roared, and we lurched off the bank toward the center of the canal. Looking back at the shore, we suddenly saw a group of about half a dozen men emerge in the clearing, all wearing similar uniforms. Some wore sun helmets, but from the distance they appeared unarmed, except possibly with side arms. It was too far to be sure.

"Sir!" shouted Queenan above the engines, "Shall we open fire? They're still in range, but won't be much longer."

For a fleeting second I thought I recognized the man who had helped me carry the girl standing in front of the group. He appeared to be given deference as a senior by the others.

"No, hold fire, they'll be out of range soon anyway."

"Okay sir, but I'd rather hit 'em out there in the open like that. They seem to think we won't shoot."

We then rounded a bend in the canal and the village dropped out of sight. About fifteen minutes later we entered the main river and turned upstream toward Sa Dec. Within a few minutes we heard the unmistakable sound of ARVN 105-mm howitzers firing. Then, still traveling at top speed, we heard the shells impacting to our rear from where we had just come.

As we powered up river at full speed, the girl, now lying wrapped in a blanket, seemed to sleep, probably after a dose of morphine. Hers was a nasty wound, and the fragment had to be removed soon. We approached the lead boat to take the doctor aboard. As the shells whined overhead, I found myself secretly hoping the man in blue would survive. I could tell he was a leader.

I later found out from intelligence that three Viet Cong battalions had met with the leaders of one North Vietnamese Army Regiment now in the area. I had indeed not been alone, and was no doubt within a hair's breadth of being captured.

Biblical Reflection

When a man finds his enemy, does he let him get away unharmed?
1 Samuel 24:19 NIV

When two armed enemies meet face to face in a time of war and consciously choose not to harm each other, what might be behind such an anomaly? A question posed thousands of years ago by an Old Testament warrior king is helpful in searching out the answer. It was King Saul who asked, "When a man finds his enemy, does he let him get away unharmed?"

After becoming Israel's first king, Saul often found himself battling his neighbors. He was able to establish himself as a warrior of renown, but with various tribal enemies around him, there was a constant need to maintain readiness and military might.

The Philistines presented particular challenges to the besieged king. The tide turned against the Philistines only when the young Israelite David defeated their formidable champion in a one-against-one contest. David continued to develop his prowess as a fighter and a leader, and eventually his military exploits surpassed Saul in the eyes of the people.

Moved by jealousy over the crowds singing, "Saul has slain his thousands, and David his ten thousands," Saul became embittered. He became the mortal enemy of David, determined to take his life. Despite the fact that they were ostensibly on the same side, David was compelled to operate with his own loyal troops to evade Saul's wrath.

One day, unexpectedly and unknowingly, Saul fell vulnerable to David. This story is recounted in 1 Samuel 24. Thinking himself quite alone, Saul had gone into a cave to relieve himself. He did not realize that David and his men were encamped further in that very cave. David's men urged him to seize and kill Saul while the opportunity was ripe. What did David do?

There are parallels between this biblical story and "Never Walk Alone." In each case military men, while meeting the demands of the day, believe they are alone. Actually, each has come under the watchful eye of the opponent. In Saul's case, as in "Never Walk Alone," the enemy came within touching distance. Saul was not aware of it at the time, but David crept close to him and cut off a piece of his robe at a very vulnerable moment. Shortly afterward David told his troops, "The LORD forbid that I should do such a thing to my master, the LORD's anointed, or lift my hand against him; for he is the anointed of the LORD" (1 Samuel 24:6 NIV). David then ordered his men not to attack or harm Saul.

After Saul left the cave, David made himself known to the king and he eloquently pleaded his case as a matter of righteousness. Saul, realizing the grave danger he had just escaped, asked the reflective question, "When a man finds his enemy, does he let him get away unharmed?" Before asking this question, he had remarked to David, "You are more righteous than I; for you have repaid me good, whereas I have repaid you evil . . . You did not kill me when the LORD put me in your hands" (1 Samuel 24:17-18).

What is the answer to Saul's question, "When a man finds his enemy, does he let him get away unharmed?" It is important to point out that though Saul and David departed from each other on that day of close encounter in the cave, and even had some sense of reconciliation, the enmity between them continued. Yet, like that February day in 1968, there was peace for the moment when two men at war with each other found common ground.

In what ways are either of these faith stories and not just the chronicling of events from two very distant conflicts? Since we do not know the faith or beliefs of the unnamed Vietnamese man in "Never Walk Alone," nor have we been made privy to the particular inner motivations of the others in the story, we are left to conjecture about the role played by faith. In David and Saul's case, we have a witness in words as to what elements of faith compelled their actions and led to Saul's penetrating question.

Saul contemplated what David had done and said much as the Vietnamese man studied the situation he came upon. Saul considered that David's words and his behavior in not killing him when he had the opportunity were words and acts of righteousness. Can such a righteous one be an enemy? In the same way, can someone rendering aid to one of my very own be my enemy? My enemy will not treat me well. Is it possible that the divine teaching, "What you do for the least of these, you do for me," resonated in a Viet Cong officer when he saw an American officer attempting to aid a wounded Vietnamese girl? How can such a person be viewed as an enemy in such a moment?

As with Saul, enmity was laid aside when God's truth was manifested between two people. Likewise, the American could have asked himself, "Will my *enemy* let me go safe?" The answer in each case is no, he will not. He who lets me go safe is not my enemy. Perhaps larger forces may compel us to contend against each other on another day, but face to face in the presence of righteous actions, there are other moral choices to be made. Where is God in such a moment? Can we know?

Unfortunately, our world is a world of war and conflict, of enmity and opposition, of antipathy and division, of the tragic reality that good and decent men and women come to face each other on the battlefield where death for some is certain. Despite remarkable advances in human community, we still solve our disputes with the flow of blood and we war with one another. In the case of David and Saul, however, recognizing the presence of God, sensing the Word of God commanding us to do justice and love mercy, and at least attempting to honor God's will in respecting life can bring moments of grace to the most harrowing conflicts for believers.

It would have been expected and obvious, perhaps, to read "Never Walk Alone" simply as an example of the blessing of the merciful. This is a good and legitimate interpretation of the story, but by focusing on the broader manifestation of God's truth in profoundly difficult moments in life, we are encouraged to formulate deeper questions, much as Saul did when he asked, "When a man finds his enemy, does he let him get away unharmed?" Such questions cause us to stop and consider that even when we are still at war there are instances that give us the hope that humanity might yet give up killing as an acceptable resolution to conflict. When one person at war has the opportunity to kill another, but sees that such a killing would be merciless and unjust, he or she is answering to a higher morality.

Theologian Karl Barth wrote of hope that is rooted in the way of the cross, in the eternal truths of God, in the way that turns humankind from bloody conflict. "Never Walk Alone" and the story of the encounter between David and Saul belong in a collection of faith stories because each reflects such eternal truths. They are faith stories, not so much about particular men, but about the presence and purpose of God in human interactions.

Dietrich Bonhoeffer was somewhat cautious of our *human* notions of eternal truth, but of the truth itself he wrote:

> "The truth shall set you free" (John 8:32). Not our deed, not our courage or strength, not our people, not our truth, but God's truth alone. Why? Because to be free does not mean to be great in the world, to be free against our brothers and sisters, to be free against God; but it means to be free from ourselves, from our untruth, in which it seems that I alone were there, as if I were the center of the world; to be free from the hatred with which I would destroy God's creation; to be free from myself in order to be free for others. God's truth alone allows me to see others. It directs my attention, bent in on myself, to what is beyond and shows me the other person. And, as it does this, I experience the love and grace of God.[1]

The sound of howitzer fire merged with the sound of boats speeding away in "Never Walk Alone." Death continued in Vietnam. Likewise, in 1 Samuel the texts tell that the conflict between Saul and David continued on another day. Eventually, the badly wounded Saul died by falling on his own sword and the Philistines cut off his head and fastened his body to the wall of Bethshan. David lived on to become king.

I cannot suggest extraordinary, supernatural intervention in either case of momentary peace; however, in a more ordinary way, I do suggest divine intervention. On two days, in two separate and distant wars, moments of peace prevailed and had meaning when men at war had moments of mutual understanding that came from recognizing and responding to the eternal truth and presence of God.

Some might draw other conclusions from "Never Walk Alone" and point to the often-recounted Old Testament stories where angels in the form of ordinary human beings lead people away from danger. We simply do not know who the

Vietnamese man may have been, but in either case, the opportunity to recognize the presence of God is the same and the mission accomplished is the same: grace and deliverance in the presence of the enemy.

CHAPTER 11

Ocean Tap

I n a bold move in October 1971, the United States government commenced planning highly secret operations to electronically tap an undersea military communications cable. The cable linked the highly sensitive Soviet Pacific submarine base and ballistic missile test range of Petropavlovsk, Kamchatka, with the Soviet mainland.

The cable, which stretched hundreds of miles at a depth of three hundred feet beneath the Sea of Okhotsk, carried highly sensitive information about Soviet Pacific Fleet submarine operations and missile tests. The Sea of Okhotsk was a particularly sensitive area. The U.S.S.R. claimed the entire sea as territorial waters, using the internationally contested "base line" method of designating territorial waters. The Soviet government had repeatedly threatened to destroy any Western units caught snooping in those waters. The tapping operation was nicknamed "Ivy Bells."

The USS *Halibut*, a nuclear submarine captained by Commander John E. McNish, was equipped with a large hanger-like pod nicknamed the "Bat Cage." The Bat Cage masqueraded as a deep-submergence research vehicle. *Halibut* planned to operate remote-control deep-sea vehicles sporting cameras capable of operating at depths up to twenty thousand feet.

In a breathtaking operation, the *Halibut* crept through the shallow entrance to the Sea of Okhotsk and commenced a covert search for the Soviet cable. The search was punctuated by brief moments of stark terror when it seemed they were about to be detected by Soviet forces; however, after days of skulking along the seabed, *Halibut* found the cable.

The next year, *Halibut* returned to the Okhotsk ocean bottom, within scant miles of the Soviet coastline and, while again avoiding detection, at the extraordinary depth of three hundred feet, launched divers who painstakingly placed electronic eavesdropping pods on the cable and then managed to reenter the Bat Cave before succumbing to the severe cold.

Over the succeeding years, special U.S. submarines continued to service the undersea pods, recovering and sending the highly sensitive tapes of Soviet voices to the super-secret National Security Agency (NSA) in Fort Meade, Maryland, for exploitation. During one servicing operation, *Halibut's* sister sub, the USS *Seawolf,* commanded by Mike Tiernan, was nearly lost while conducting follow-up servicing operations on the cable. Tethered to the ocean bottom when a highly unusual storm broke over the Sea of Okhotsk, *Seawolf* was repeatedly slammed so violently into the seabed that she barely escaped alive.

The sea tapping operations were so lucrative to U.S. intelligence interests that an additional tap was planned in 1986, to be carried out by a new and more sophisticated submarine, the USS *Parche.* The target this time was a Soviet undersea cable in the highly dangerous waters of the Soviet Northern Fleet, home of the Soviet Navy's largest and most modern submarines.

On the eve of the Reykjavik Summit, just as planning for the new tap was going into the final stages, the FBI revealed—to the horror of U.S. officials—that Ronald Pelton, an NSA employee, had been spying for the Soviet Union and had passed information compromising the Sea of Okhotsk tap. Shocked U.S. intelligence officials watched with sinking spirits as they saw on satellite imagery a group of Soviet naval and deep-sea diving ships hovering off the exact spot where *Halibut* and associates had tapped the Sea of Okhotsk cable. The Soviets actually retrieved the tap pods and later displayed them in the Cold War Intelligence Museum in KGB Headquarters at Moscow's Lubyanka prison.

Nevertheless, the crew of the USS *Parche* found and tapped the northern cable and the tap remained secure. From this daring move came some of the most valuable intelligence ever collected electronically during the Cold War—intelligence that contributed to the successful conclusion of the Intermediate-range Nuclear Forces (INF) Treaty negotiations.

These hair-raising operations were conducted by the men of the U.S. submarine force, in submarines equipped with destructive explosives designed to destroy both the submarine and all hands on board should they be discovered and confronted by Soviet anti-submarine forces. That these operations continued until the end of the Cold War is a tribute to the men of the "silent service." Although these were some of the most daring operations ever conducted, they were unknown to all but a few in the higher echelons of power.

Biblical Reflection

I tell you the truth, whatever you did for one of the least of these brothers of mine, you did for me. Matthew 25:40 NIV

In the shelter of your presence you hide them from the intrigues of men; in your dwelling you keep them safe from accusing tongues. Psalm 31:20 NIV

The Cold War was filled with suspicions, hostile tensions, and crises that could all too easily lead to full-scale armed conflict between Soviet Bloc nations and Western democracies. The Cuban Missile Crisis of 1962 and the Soviet invasion of Afghanistan in 1979 are two clear examples of situations that might have resulted in global warfare. Due in part, however, to intelligence operations that provided information on important developments in time to counteract possible devastating consequences, the world was not plunged into catastrophe.

Of course, proxy wars did occur during the Cold War, and other serious, danger-laden situations arose, but those in the service of protecting peace and freedom worked on behalf of the world to avert worst-case scenarios. The individual sacrifices on both sides of the Cold War may never be fully known.

Tensions between rival peoples and uneasy peace accords extend as far back as the beginnings of recorded history. Joshua 22 details the story of a war that was barely averted when two formerly allied groups divided territory between them and then found themselves embroiled in religious and ideological disputes. One group armed itself and actually marshaled forces for war against the other.

After successfully waging a very long campaign as allies, the several tribes under Joshua's leadership were finally able to declare a victory against their common enemies. The tribes of Reuben, Gad, and the half-tribe of Manasseh were given lands in Gilead on one side of the Jordan River while their brother tribes, which made up the army of Israel, were granted possession of lands on the other side of the river.

Trouble arose when the Reubenites, the Gadites, and the half-tribe of Manasseh erected a large altar in Canaan. This was viewed as such an offense by the rest of Israel that they began war preparations at Shiloh, where the tribes had just separated as allies and friends.

Before the planned attack, the Israelites sent a delegation consisting of ten high officials. Led by the priest Phinehas, the delegates from Israel explained exactly why the altar might lead to war. Sacrifices and offerings to God were to be made only at the altar of the Lord that stood before the tabernacle that held the Ark of the Covenant. The Israelites feared that should burnt offerings or sacrifices be offered at a different altar it would offend God and turn God against them.

The talks proved very fruitful. The Reubenites and company were able to prove they meant no offense Their only intention in building the altar was to memorialize the relationship between the two groups in their mutual service to God. They had no intention of using it as a place for burnt offerings and sacrifices. Certain war was averted when each side understood the other's real intentions.

Soviet and Western nations did not have the advantage of the ancient tribes in the Joshua story, which were close allies before the trouble began. World War II was the occasion for a very uneasy alliance among these ideological opposites. After the war, averting new wars and disasters was not as simple and straightforward as simply meeting at the negotiation table to come to friendly and mutual understandings. It called for covert information gathering and constant watchfulness.

The submarine crews gathered information at extreme personal risk. Few know their names, and their accomplishments were often, of necessity, kept entirely secret. Nevertheless, they served with courage. Every day people perform selfless deeds for others and we who benefit remain unaware that through their efforts the Lord provides for us all. It is the Lord himself who declared, "Whatever you did for the least of these, you did for me."

CHAPTER 12

Boat People

My last involvement with Vietnamese events, following three years in and around Indochina, occurred in 1978, while I was serving as a ship's officer aboard the aircraft carrier USS *Enterprise*. The ship was operating out of Subic Bay in the Philippines, heading for the Indian Ocean via Malacca.

One night, while conducting exercises in the Philippine Sea, a surveillance aircraft reported a small craft drifting in moderate seas with about twenty people aboard. It was a motorized junk heavily laden with people seeking new life elsewhere. *Enterprise* followed standing fleet orders regarding encounters with the many frantic refugees from Vietnam, prosaically called "Vietnamese boat people."

This was the bottom line of the Vietnam War, the one not recognized by those who advocated abandoning the Vietnamese to their own fate. The fleet orders were to render assistance only if human lives were in danger. As a Vietnamese language speaker, I was directed by the commanding officer to be present at the starboard gangway when we took the junk alongside to evaluate the situation.

A detachment of marines led by a young lieutenant waited with me as the overladen and wallowing craft rowed in to the brightly illuminated accommodation ladder. An aircraft carrier the size of *Enterprise*, looming more than eighty feet overhead, is a bewildering sight for the uninitiated. The lieutenant and I descended the swaying ladder to inspect the boat. The marine party assigned to investigate the craft with me communicated with the ship's bridge via sound-powered phones.

"The captain wants a report on the condition of the people in the boat," a voice shouted down the ladder.

The lieutenant and I, wearing bulky kapok life jackets, reached the bottom of the long accommodation ladder and peered into the boat. The situation was grim. The boat was out of fuel, overcrowded, with only inches of freeboard showing. If the weather worsened only slightly the craft would certainly founder. The scene was familiar. It was like looking deep into my past. Even the smell was the same: fish sauce and beetle nut. Twenty-three Vietnamese of every age huddled in the boat, eyes wide with fright.

"Sir, the captain wants to know how many souls aboard," a marine shouted down the ladder.

"Twenty-three, counting three babies and five children."

"What's their condition?"

"Wet, cold, and scared."

"What's the condition of the boat?"

"Engine quit, no fuel."

"Captain wants to know if the people are in danger." I looked at the lieutenant, too young to have been in Vietnam.

"Sir, we have to unload the boat to look at the condition of the hull and to see what's wrong with the engine. Tell the bosuns to send down some gasoline."

The Vietnamese streamed up the ladder. Several more marines came down to help carry the children. With the boat empty, the lieutenant and I took the Vietnamese leader back onto the junk to inspect the engine. The swells sent water cascading into the boat. It looked hopeless. Even if they could get the motor running well enough to make headway, the boat would certainly not make the nearest landfall with more than twenty people aboard. It was cold and, after standing in the wet hull for a few minutes, we were soaked through.

"Sir, the captain wants to know the condition of the boat."

"Send up for a fire axe," I told the lieutenant. We motioned for the Vietnamese man to leave the boat, and he lost no time scrambling up the ladder. A long-handled red fire axe came down the ladder, passed hand to hand by the marines. The lieutenant handed it to me.

"What are you going to do with that, sir?"

"Turn away," I answered. "Sometimes things need to be done without asking permission." I swung the axe several times at the transom of the junk and knocked the engine into the water.

"Get back on the ladder," I shouted to the marine, and gave the hull several whacks with the axe. Seawater began to gush into the hull. Happily, no one could see the junk beneath the overhang of the flight deck, including the ship's executive officer (XO), who had finally joined the group at the top of the accommodation ladder. He stood nervously directing the activity sixty feet above the junk.

"Boat's sinking," I shouted, then jumped onto the ladder's platform. The lieutenant grabbed my arm to steady me. I cut the line holding the junk to the ship. The rapidly sinking hulk drifted away from the side of the steel giant and was soon totally awash.

The lieutenant let me know that the XO wanted an explanation about what doing with the axe. I looked at the lieutenant, whose eyes brightened with sudden enlightenment. "What axe?" I shouted back, and slid the fire axe into the water, watching it drop from sight into the dark sea.

We climbed up the ladder and looked down. The junk capsized and drifted away into the night.

The XO was suddenly standing in front of me, demanding to know what had happened.

"Well, sir," I began, "we were trying to fix the engine and she began to sink."

The XO questioned what I was doing with the fire axe. I looked at the young lieutenant, who appeared frightened, wondering if I would lie to the XO. "Sir, you know I used to be a chief engineer on a destroyer and spent a year on the Mekong River climbing on and off those Vietnamese junks. I know how temperamental Vietnamese gas engines can be. Was just using the axe to try and fix it, sir."

"Where's the axe?" he responded.

"I must have dropped it while evacuating the boat, sir."

"Captain," he said into the phone, "this is the XO. The junk sank. The refugees are on their way to sick bay for a medical check. I'll have the main galley bring hot soup and tea to sick bay." The XO looked at me, shook his head, and made his way back to the bridge to join the captain.

Biblical Reflection

"Because the poor are despoiled, because the needy groan, I will now rise up," says the Lord; "I will place them in the safety for which they long." Psalm 12:5

Refuge sought and refuge given is a recurring theme throughout the Bible. This is particularly the case in the book of Psalms, which also provides stark depictions of oppression and oppressors. For example in Psalm 10:8-10 we read:

> They sit in ambush in the villages;
> in hiding places they murder the innocent.
> Their eyes stealthily watch for the helpless;
> they lurk in secret like a lion in its covert;
> they lurk that they may seize the poor;
> they seize the poor and drag them off in their net.
> They stoop, they crouch,
> and the helpless fall by their might.

In the wake of U.S. withdrawal after the war, countless Vietnamese citizens were victimized in the very ways described in the Psalm 10. Imprisonment, murder, forced indoctrination in reeducation camps, deprivation, and horrible abuses of basic human rights were the norm rather than the exception. Those who dared and were able took to the sea in any available vessel rather than remain and face the brutality and chaos at home.

Historians report that *most* who tried to escape by sea were lost. Some fell victim to pirates, some starved, some succumbed to dehydration or disease, and a great number drowned. Despite the large numbers lost, however, many refugees survived the remarkable hardships and eventually found the safety they sought.

In the early 1990s, I was privileged to teach refugee children in a middle school in San Diego. They came with faces full of determination and bodies tense with memories of the unique experiences that had brought them to a foreign shore. As students, many achieved brilliant successes, tackling the twin hurdles of a new language and culture while their families struggled with difficult economic challenges. They were among the modern-day "groaning and despoiled poor" who managed to find opportunities for themselves in new countries around the world.

That particular day when twenty-three souls were taken on board the USS *Enterprise* could be described from any number of perspectives. One could describe the moment in terms of U.S. policy. One could describe it from the personal point of view of any of the individuals directly involved as rescuers. One could certainly ask for the point of view of any of the desperate people on board the makeshift vessel who were old enough to remember the ordeal. One could describe it in ways that totally leave God out of the picture, but I cannot. Nor can I leave God out of the picture when thinking of those whose lives were lost at sea. They matter too. They are counted among the despoiled poor who have God's attention.

God is concerned with humankind. His great desire is that we be servants of one another and not despoilers. God would like an end to horrible, inhumane policies and practices that make helpless people so desperate they are willing to risk their lives trying to escape.

God calls humanity to live together in righteousness, though we all too often fail to obey this call. Righteousness is not some vague concept developed by sanctimonious pundits of religion. Righteousness flows from practicing justice, mercy, and humility, each a tremendously demanding concept. The costs of serving justice and mercy are constant costs. Sometimes the price involves giving up one's own life or freedom to secure life and freedom for others. The price always involves thoughtful consideration of appropriate action. The humility demanded of us is that we recognize our responsibilities as creatures of a maker who designed us for deep fellowship with him and with one another, our rebellion, greed, and oppression notwithstanding.

In the case of the Vietnamese boat people, I am reminded of the psalmist's declaration in Psalm 18:16-19:

> He reached down from on high, he took me;
> he drew me out of mighty waters.
> He delivered me from my strong enemy,
> and from those who hated me;
> for they were too mighty for me.
> They confronted me in the day of my calamity;
> but the LORD was my support.
> He brought me out into a broad place;
> he delivered me, because he delighted in me.

What I know is that I delighted in—and remember the names and faces of—the refugee children who came to be my students. These children owed their lives to the daring of others who were instrumental in their escape and rescue. I remember the shared smiles in my classroom as they learned the language and culture that would open new doors of hope for them. I am grateful to God for the lives of those children.

I am also glad for the determination to rescue the help-less that prevailed on board *Enterprise* and other ships that became places of refuge for those who otherwise were almost certain to be lost. Whether the crews acknowledge it or not, the will of God was done with each rescue—as it is any time justice and mercy are served.

CHAPTER 13

The Second Oldest Profession

I n the serene beauty of the southern Montenegro coast
near the Port of Tivat, a ship repair facility squats near
the entrance to the historic Bay of Kotor. This deep and
protected harbor already occupied a celebrated place in
naval history as the homeport for the once powerful fleet of
the Austrian-Hungarian Empire before its implosion in World
War I.

In the 1980s, the then-Yugoslav shipyard repaired Soviet,
Libyan, and occasionally other foreign warships. During the
1970s and 80s, there were often three Soviet naval ships there,
a submarine tender and two Foxtrot-class diesel submarines
undergoing routine re-fit. Libya also maintained two of their
Soviet-built submarines in Tivat for routine overhaul. Therefore, at any given time from 1980 to 1984 there would be four
Soviet-made submarines in Tivat.

The U.S. Navy tried to cite the regular presence of Soviet
and Libyan submarines in Tivat as evidence that Yugoslavia
was stretching its nonalignment status. The Yugoslav Navy,
however, skillfully argued that these warships were allowed
in Tivat by the Yugoslav law governing territorial waters
and the presence of foreign warships in their ports. This law
defined the total tonnage, number of ships, and the length
of time foreign warships could visit Yugoslav ports at the
same time.

That period saw an increasing number of incidents
between the U.S. Navy and Libya over excessive Libyan

claims regarding the extent of territorial waters in the Gulf of Sirte, as well as from Libyan support for international terrorism. Libya was a key ally of Yugoslavia, employing thousands of Yugoslav engineers. In return, the Yugoslav armed forces trained hundreds of Libyans at their bases and facilities.

Each time a crisis occurred in the Mediterranean between the United States and Libya, the U.S. Navy alerted the Belgrade attaché office to conduct an immediate reconnaissance of Libyan diesel submarines in Tivat. Given the reckless nature of Colonel Qaddafi's use of his Soviet weapons systems, and since he possessed six former Soviet long-range diesel attack submarines in varying states of readiness, the U.S. fleet was very attentive to Libyan movements.

The Libyan submarines carried torpedoes and presented a real threat despite their usual poor state of material readiness. Since one-third of the Libyan submarine fleet was normally in the Balkan backyard of Tivat, the Western attachés in Belgrade were ordered repeatedly to report on short notice: How many Libyan ships are in Tivat? Are they ready for sea? Do they have torpedoes aboard?

Tivat lies about seven hundred kilometers due south of Belgrade across the formidable mountain barriers of Montenegro. In good weather it was possible to reach Tivat by car in twelve to sixteen hours. It was a long distance, but when the navy called the attachés acted. With the assistance of a closely-knit allied attaché group, they devised a watch system whereby one attaché was always ready to leave for Tivat at a moment's notice.

Using agreed-upon intelligence gathering procedures, the attachés were able to put their report on the wire and out to the fleet within minutes of completing their reconnaissance. They certainly violated every security regulation governing the use of telephones in a communist country, but they accomplished the mission and never used the same routine twice. The U.S. Sixth Fleet generally knew from the Belgrade-based naval attachés whether the Libyans were in port or not and whether there were any major repairs underway, which could indicate the state of their readiness for sea.

During one particularly strained period, it appeared the Libyan submarines were scrambling to depart Tivat early. At the same time, one of the Sixth Fleet's aircraft carriers was visiting Venice at the top of the Adriatic Sea. To keep track of Libyan activity, two NATO attachés spent an entire week drifting from one Dalmatian bed and breakfast to another, each overlooking the visible channel from Tivat to the open Adriatic, waiting to report the submarines' departure. The scenario of a Libyan submarine lying in ambush behind one of the fourteen hundred Yugoslav Adriatic islands for a nuclear-powered carrier had the makings of a Tom Clancy techno-thriller.

Although the mission was demanding, the setting could not have been more beautiful. The Montenegrin and Bosnian coasts surrounding the towns of Herzegnovi and Tivat are magnificent. The attachés often climbed high above the breathtaking Bay of Kotor, permeated with the aroma of mimosa, and watched the islands stretching far out in the azure Adriatic. It was a paradisiacal setting for a job, one which seemed a bit unlikely in the nuclear age.

The U.S. attaché devised a practical solution to this demanding intelligence-gathering task by recruiting a local informer. By good fortune, the attaché met a Yugoslav who worked in the Tivat shipyard as a foreman directing the repair work on Libyan submarines. The attaché set up a reporting network with this invaluable source, a young Jewish Bosnian from Sarajevo named Jacob, who was fervently anti-Libyan.

Thus, with very little cost, the attaché obtained timely and accurate information directly from a source on the scene and forwarded it swiftly to the fleet. The scheme was practical, but not without its tense moments. Once while discreetly passing the weekly Tivat shipyard maintenance schedule to the attaché in a crowded restaurant in Belgrade's bohemian Skadarlia district, the young Bosnian was set upon by several rowdy Serbs stoked with too much *slivovitz*, the local plum spirit. Fearing they had been caught in the act of espionage, the two fled in opposite directions. Later they realized their assailants had attacked merely because they saw the informant's Star of David hanging from a chain around his neck. No amount of counsel could deter the young Jew from sporting his talisman. From that time on, however, as a precaution when in Belgrade he wore it beneath his shirt. Needless to say, the handoff of information was always a tense affair.

In one typical night encounter, the attaché moved quietly along the wet cobblestones down the winding, dark Belgrade streets, the smell of garlic, *slivovitz,* and tobacco strong in the night air. He stepped behind an empty kiosk, convinced that a single figure was coming up on him from behind. After waiting for a few moments, he continued in the direction of the river, toward the foot of the crumbling walls of the old fortress *Kalamegdan.* He slipped quietly into the shelter of a doorway and waited.

Belgrade in a late autumn rain is as cold as the dead. The shadow of the fortress loomed dark over the narrow street. The attaché stiffened as a shadowy figure from behind him paused. Surveillance had been heavy recently and it was becoming more difficult to make the trip from the diplomatic quarter in Dedinje to the lower Belgrade riverfront squalor and stench below Kalamegdan without picking up foot surveillance. He was used to vehicular surveillance; that was normal for attachés. This was far more difficult.

Despite his careful movements, he had picked up some kind of shadow, either Serb police or military counterintelligence—he didn't know which. It didn't really matter much; they were all equally ruthless, unprincipled, and out of control. The American was tired from the long trip from Sarajevo, but he would have to shake his follower. He squeezed further into the urine-stinking doorway and listened. "Can't see you, mister, but I can feel you," he thought, as he sensed a figure approaching. He froze as the form moved past. It was silent again. The sound of a riverboat below on the Danube drifted above the silence. The American came out of the doorway and quietly walked in the opposite direction. Jacob would be waiting by the side of the old fortress, nervous and edgy. He had only an hour before he was due to deliver the submarine repair status report to the Libyan People's Bureau in central Belgrade.

On that particular night, when the attaché opened Jacob's envelope he found the blueprints of the entire Tivat shipyard along with the schedule for the repair of Libyan and Soviet subs for the next six months. Jacob had proven himself to be reliable, exact, and extremely dedicated. His devotion in subverting the Libyans, in fact, was extreme to the point of becoming a danger to himself. Once, when Jacob's comely sister substituted for him at a rendezvous with the American attaché, she explained that her firebrand brother had attacked two Libyan sailors at Herzegnovi near Tivat after they had made a pass at her.

The information Jacob provided proved valuable and accurate in every case. It was a glorious arrangement. A delighted Sixth Fleet intelligence officer learned the precise sailing dates of the Libyan submarines, and the attaché parted with a great deal of American bourbon and sleep on the harrowing late night trips to the squalid Belgrade riverfront.

Despite the difficulties and danger, the reporting arrangement lasted more than a year, and then abruptly ended. Jacob again sent his sister to meet the attaché in Belgrade to pass on what would be his last report. Near tears, the dark-eyed beauty explained that her explosive brother had bashed another sailor with a wrench, this time a Libyan officer. Jacob had fled the area and made his way south, where he left Yugoslavia via the ferry from nearby Bar across to Bari, Italy. He then made his way to join the Israeli Army. While the U.S. Navy lost a good intelligence source, the Israelis certainly gained a determined scrapper.

Biblical Reflection

When David came to the summit, where God was worshiped, Hushai the Archite came to meet him with his coat torn and earth on his head. David said to him, "If you go on with me, you will be a burden to me. But if you return to the city and say to Absalom, 'I will be your servant, O king; as I have been your father's servant in time past, so now I will be your servant,' then you will defeat for me the counsel of Ahithophel. The priests Zadok and Abiathar will be with you there. So whatever you hear from the king's house, tell it to the priests Zadok and Abiathar. Their two sons are with them there, Zadok's son Ahimaaz and Abiathar's son Jonathan; and by them you shall report to me everything you hear." 2 Samuel 15:32-36

Zadok was the chief priest in King David's court and Ahimaaz was his son. Both men served David as spies and were involved in saving the king's life when his own son, Absalom, rose up against him in revolt. The saga of the entire conspiracy is set out in 2 Samuel 15–19, where we learn that the web of people engaged in espionage for both sides clearly influenced the outcomes.

The questions the spies sought to answer were similar to those recorded in "The Second Oldest Profession." How many? What are their weapons? Where can they be found? Who are the messengers? What will the signals be? The writer of 2 Samuel tells of treachery, courage, and ultimate triumph for David due to the work of those who gathered information for him.

For many complex reasons, Absalom was alienated from his father. He conspired with Ahitophel, one of David's trusted counselors, in an attempt to overthrow his father. They sent secret messengers to help spread word of the coup attempt. David learned of this and charged Hushai, another advisor, to pretend to go over to Absalom's side. Hushai was then to inform Zadok, Ahimaaz, and Jonathan, David's uncle, of any developments.

Hushai was faithful in his role and made sure David was protected from the plans being hatched against him. The risk to all the spies was great. Ahimaaz and Jonathan took measures to avoid being detected. They used a maid to carry messages between themselves and Hushai. A young boy, however, discovered their method and reported them to Absalom.

Absalom immediately sent his men in pursuit and David's agents had to hide to save their lives. They found shelter in a well and were helped by a woman who spread a covering over the mouth of the well and disguised it with piles of grain. The woman told Absalom's men she had seen Jonathan and Ahimaaz going over the brook. Her ruse worked, and the lives of the spies were saved. They were able to reach David in time to report to him the strategies and positions of his enemies. David prevailed, though his son was lost in the ensuing battle. Then said Ahimaaz the son of Zadok, "Let me run and carry tidings to the king that the Lord has delivered him from the power of his enemies." And Joab said to him, "You are not to carry tidings today; you may carry tidings another day, but today you shall carry no tidings, because the king's son is dead." Then Ahimaaz the son of Zadok said again to Joab, "Come what may, let me also run after the Cushite." And Joab said, "Why will you run, my son, seeing that you will have no reward for the tidings?" "Come what may," he said, "I will run."

CHAPTER 14

Escape to Freedom

Jan Smid lived in Bratislava, Czechoslovakia, and held a coveted doctorate in mathematics from Prague University. His dream of using his skills on space research was as remote as the dreams of so many for real freedom in Eastern Europe in the mid-1980s. Recognizing his keen talent, the Czech regime gave Jan work in a defense plant building anti-aircraft missile warheads for the Soviet Army. Jan's wife, Blanca, was a graduate dental student and worked after classes for the Czech Ministry of Health. The couple had two young children.

Being of exceptional talent, and as a reward for good work habits, Jan was granted a travel permit, called a gray passport, that allowed him to vacation with his family each year outside of Czechoslovakia, but not in the West. Since he worked in a sensitive industry, he could travel only to the socialist countries of Yugoslavia and Romania, where he and his family were allowed to enjoy the luxury of relaxing by the sea.

They first visited Yugoslavia in 1981, driving their basic Skoda twin cylinder across the Bosnian mountains to camp along the Adriatic coast in Croatia. For Eastern Europeans at that time, life in Yugoslavia was relatively free and the Smid family was able to spend time on the seaside with little or no interference from security police. It was here, in a small Yugoslav town where I was waiting for the car ferry to the island of Korchula, that I first met the Smid family. On leave from the Belgrade embassy, I was on my way to visit Yugo-slav friends on that picturesque island.

I first discovered the depth of Jan's desire to visit and work in the free world while talking with him on the pier waiting to cross to Korchula. His dreams of working as an engineer on space exploration were real and not merely fantasy. I invited Jan to visit my seaside retreat on the island where I stayed when on leave. The stone cottage where I stayed belonged to an old war hero nicknamed Pershona, an 85-year-old former leader of a communist Partisan company in the bloody gue-rilla war against the Nazi occupiers. (You will find more of his story in "The Old Croat.")

Jan agreed to visit, but only after dark since, because of his work, he was forbidden to speak with Westerners, let alone Western diplomats, or even worse, military diplomats. Understandably, he wished not to be observed. In our con-versation, it soon became clear that Jan and his wife were carefully planning to escape across the northern border of Yugoslavia into Italy. His scheme was still in the formative stage when he asked if he might visit me in Belgrade on his way back to Bratislava. I agreed, but I made it clear that as a military diplomat I was unable to openly assist him with his escape plans.

Two weeks later Jan called me in Belgrade, and as before, wished to visit after dark. That evening he drove his little Skoda up the hill to Dedinje, an upscale Belgrade neighbor-hood where some embassies were located. Jan parked his car in what he thought was a secure spot and walked to my resi-dence. I later learned that he had parked his car in front of the home of Colonel Arkady Zhuk, the Soviet military attaché.

Over the next two years, Jan and his family made several more visits to Yugoslavia, ostensibly for vacation but really to continue their detailed reconnaissance of the northern Cro-atian and Slovenian borders with Italy. He met with me once again in Belgrade and asked if he might, on a subsequent visit, give me a package of personal papers for safekeeping.

In the early summer of 1984, while heading to the coast from the Czech border, Jan brought me a package containing his university diploma, doctorate, birth certificates, and other personal papers. He wished me farewell and said proudly that the next time I heard from him they would be in the West. I wished him good fortune.

Less than a year later, after I had returned to the United States and was assigned in Washington, D.C, I received an international telephone call from Jan. "We're in Rome," he said happily. "We made it!"

Within two months he had cleared through immigration with the assistance of the Tolstoy Foundation, which helped talented escapees from the East enter the United States and find work. This is the story of their escape:

Since I had last seen him, Jan had made two additional visits to the Dalmatian coast on his gray passport and had attended one conference for international mathematicians in Zagreb, Croatia. Driving along the Croatian seacoast and into Slovenia near Trieste, he discovered several ski resorts that kept their lifts running in summer so tourists could ascend to trek in the eastern Dolomites. The area was a popular spot for visitors and it would be especially easy for the Smids to blend in with the many tourists from all over the world.

One day in July 1984, the Smids hid their car in the woods near the base of a ski lift not far from Nova Goritsa, bought tickets for the lift, and rode to the top of the green ski slopes. They dismounted and began to climb toward the peak. There were other climbers, trekkers, and strollers around so the young family did not attract undue attention. That is, until they achieved the ridgeline.

There were signs warning wanderers to keep away from the frontier, as Italy lay on just the other side of the mountain. Jan led his family up the trail running along the ridge. When they were near the end of the path, which was marked with wire and more signs to keep away, Jan took his two-year-old son in his arms, and with his wife Blanca taking the daughter, climbed under the wire. Suddenly they heard a shout: "*Stoj!*" (Stop!)

Jan looked back and saw three Yugoslav border guards dressed in gray about three hundred meters away on the path. One carried an automatic weapon while the others had side arms. They motioned for the Smid family to stop where they were. One fired a burst from his automatic weapon into the air for emphasis.

The family froze for a brief moment, and then Jan said quietly, "Quickly, do as I do and stay with me. Don't look back." Holding his son, he began to run and then jumped down the steep edge of the mountain, which was mostly dirt and gravel at that height. He sensed Blanca and his daughter right behind him. He landed on his backside, and slid swiftly down the slope. He heard several shots ring out above. At first he was close to panic, but Jan was enough of a hunter to realize that at that range moving targets would be difficult to hit. The family of four slid all the way down into Italy and freedom, the only casualty the seats of their pants.

Biblical Reflection

An angel of the Lord appeared to Joseph in a dream and said, "Get up, take the child and his mother, and flee to Egypt." Matthew 2:13

To rise up, take their children, and flee is a longing in the hearts of countless men and women who are in danger and seeking justice and safety for themselves and their families. Not all are able to answer that longing and yet whenever anyone is able to escape to freedom the rest of the world is enriched. Jan and Blanca's escape to freedom and the witness of what they accomplished are powerful. Their story resonates with familiar biblical texts.

In the days of Herod, king of Judea, a child was born in Bethlehem to a young woman named Mary. The story of her son, Jesus, has changed the world. Though little is known of Jesus' childhood, and although not much beyond genealogy and a few brief events are recorded about his family, some pivotal details are provided in the biblical record. For instance, Joseph, Mary's husband, was a just man, a carpenter by trade, and a man unwilling to see his wife brought to harm. He demonstrated his protective nature time and again.

What possible things would a highly trained modern mathematician, possibly an atheist, and the carpenter Joseph, who lived thousands of years ago, have in common? What threads might connect their stories? The obvious things are simple. Both men are husbands and fathers and both occupy themselves with gainful work, as they are able. Both men devote themselves to the women and children they love. As with other men, both Jan and Joseph dream dreams and have visions for the future. They both took bold steps to attain their dreams.

It is simply unremarkable that the carpenter Joseph, husband of Mary, and the mathematician Jan, husband of Blanca, share these traits. And although heroic, it is not surprising that women like Blanca and Mary also seized the opportunity to nurture and protect the lives of their families despite great risks.

Though the holy family's story is unique in history for other reasons, there are situations embedded in these two stories that make them startlingly similar. The inspiration to flee and the compelling reasons to flee bear searching out in both stories.

In one story an angel appears and speaks the Word of God, which compels Joseph, Mary, and the child Jesus to flee from danger. In the other story, a man and his wife successfully develop and execute a careful plan to escape danger and seek a better life. Must we leave God out of the second story?

Let's first focus on the settings in which each story occurs. In each case, conditions exist in which rulers practice harsh suppression and even harsher punishment. Despotic leaders had—and have—little accountability for their atrocious acts. History records Herod's ruthless and demented paranoia as he slew one member of his own family after another. Modern accounts of the victims of the Soviet machinery are incomplete, and yet stories of countless lives and dreams lost to the inhumanity and deprivations of communism are rampant.

Joseph fled to save the life of Jesus. Even if Herod's order to his soldiers to go through Bethlehem and kill all male infants under two years of age is only recorded in the book of Matthew, Herod's other cruelties and ambitions are well documented and his character as a leader is clear. To remove one's family from his reach was prudent, to say the least. Joseph's goal was to find a better and safer place for his family than under the tyranny of this dangerous man.

Jan Smid wanted to flee to a life of freedom from oppression. His entire family defied death under a hail of bullets. And whether killing the bodies or attempting to kill the spirits of their people, the Herods of history continue on in many guises. The ambitions and cruelties of corrupt governments and the slaughter and oppression of the innocent continue in an almost unabated march through time.

Both the story of the family of Jesus and the story of the Smid family demonstrate that individual people do matter, especially in the chaos of violence and oppression. And because Matthew recorded the story of "the slaughter of the innocents," it is driven home to us that among the individuals who matter are the innocents who are lost and remain unnamed for us. They matter to us. As people hearing the stories recounted above, we are moved to mourn those who are victimized by tyranny and oppression while we celebrate the escapes of those who dare to seek safety and freedom.

The question remains, however: does God care? Of course, it may seem a ridiculous question in reference to Jesus to ask, "Does God care?" And what of Jan, Blanca, and their children? Could not this text from Job also speak to their situation?

For God does speak—now one way, now another—though
man may not perceive it. In a dream, in a vision of the
night, when deep sleep falls on men as they slumber in
their beds, he may speak in their ears and terrify them with
warnings. Job 33:14-16 NIV

I do not know Jan or Blanca Smid, and I do not know the
details of their decision to flee Yugoslavia for the freedom of
the West, so let us instead rivet our attention on one small
story in Matthew's Gospel, that of the "slaughter of the innocents." How might this story help us to answer the question,
"Does God care?"

As pointed out above, nowhere except in the Gospel of
Matthew is the slaughter of the innocents recorded. Perhaps
historians of the time considered the deaths of a relatively
small number of children in Bethlehem of little note in the
dark history of Herod's cruelty. Could it be, however, that
Matthew saw fit to record the story to remind us that the
death of the innocent does not escape the attention of God?
The escape of Joseph, Mary, and Jesus from Herod's tyranny
sheds the light of divine judgment on that tyranny and witnesses to the lives of those who did not escape. Cannot the
same be said of the Smid family's escape from tyranny?

Few of us today know the specifics of the crushed dreams
and lost lives of those countless people fed to the Gulags—
places of terror and suffering spawned by the greed and
unconcern of oppressive governments. Somehow though, the
triumphs of the few who escape to freedom become triumphs
for all because they bear witness for those left behind. It is no
accident that their stories come to light. For both Joseph the
carpenter and Jan the mathematian, could it not be said: "In
his heart a man plans his course, but the LORD determines his
steps" (Proverbs 16:9 NIV)?

CHAPTER 15

God in Romania

I n countries that maintain complete centralized control over information and where defense developments are tightly wrapped in secrecy, Western diplomats, and especially military attachés, are forced to travel a great deal. As Ambassador David Funderfurk said in 1982 to his staff at the U.S. Embassy in Bucharest, Romania, "Get out and get the feel of the people."

Travel enabled firsthand observation of what in more open countries could be culled from the pages of the open press. In the West, information concerning new trends in the economy, agriculture, maritime and naval construction, weapons, and policy is available in military circles and open to the international press. Attachés, like journalists, make their living on the flow of information. During the Cold War, Romania was among the Eastern countries where it was most difficult to obtain military information.

Romania was firmly in the grip of its state security organization, the Securitate. Information concerning the most trivial aspect of defense was hermetically sealed from foreigners. Tourist maps of Romania were altered to hide military bases. Objects such as bridges, communications facilities, public transportation, power plants, and ports were designated strategic objects and placed on a list of locations forbidden to foreign observation and photography. Defense authorities censored all information appearing in the press pertaining to military developments.

For those reasons, the naval attaché resident in Belgrade, and dually accredited in Romania, timed frequent visits to Bucharest to coincide with the Romanian national and military holidays. By doing so, the attaché gained maximum exposure to senior Romanian military officers and high-level government officials.

Three major information objectives during that period were: (1) to uncover the flourishing Romanian Navy ship-building program, (2) to disclose the true interface of the Romanian military machine with the Soviet defense forces, and (3) to debunk the publicly stated deceit that Romania prohibited transit of Soviet and other Warsaw Pact forces across its territory.

The Romanians were adept at concealing their military bases from the general public and foreign attachés. They used movable walls to mask building projects from the open roads. The attaché was thus forced to insert himself into areas off the public roads, by car or by foot. This meant extracting from the area without being observed or, worse, being stopped and identified by nervous guards. Therefore, the value of the observation effort had to be weighed quickly against the risk of identification, exposure, and detention by the local security.

U.S. sailors acquitted themselves well during this period of the Cold War when the fleet made port visits to Yugoslavia and Romania. Many foreign service officers often doubted the value of these visits. They were, however, highly significant in these two countries during the height of the Cold War when the United States affirmed the independence of the breakaway communist state, Yugoslavia, and applauded the Warsaw Pact maverick, Romania. These ship visits enabled the United States to "show the flag" and put thousands of American sailors ashore among the captive communist populations.

In addition to the major political role played by the navy visits, they presented an opportunity during otherwise isolated duty for the U.S. attaché to meet the officers and men of the fleet. It was also an opportunity for the attaché to brief the flag officers and their staffs from the perspective of his diplomatic and regional expertise.

Arranging and carrying out a successful ship visit was a considerable challenge for an attaché serving in a totally closed society, where normal domestic products were scarce. In his hands rested the responsibility to set the stage for the visits with the host navies. In particular, he had to guarantee navigational safety in spite of the fact that local navigational charts were often considered secret by the host countries.

The attaché arranged security and protocol schedules, as well as sporting and entertainment events for the crew. Visits to Western countries were trying enough, but in closed societies that sheltered their populations from the visitors, the job could be frustrating and sometimes infuriating. The attaché's greatest fear was that a well-meaning but careless act would precipitate a damaging incident.

Many years in the navy taught that when things went wrong in the fleet they could go extraordinarily wrong. During this Cold War period of port visits for the U.S. Navy in Yugoslavia, Romania, and finally in the Soviet Union, however, there was never a serious case of misconduct on the part of American sailors. This is a tribute not only to the leadership of the officers and petty officers of today's fleet who prepared their men and women for these important visits, but also to the quality of the modern American sailor. The young Americans, from small towns in the Midwest to inner-city Brooklyn, conducted themselves with great credit while on independent liberty in these communist countries, where the average citizen enjoyed far fewer freedoms than they did.

During this period the U.S. Navy played an especially effective role as a versatile instrument of U.S. foreign policy. The role of the navy as a direct tool of diplomacy has a long history that has not diminished with the proliferation of diplomatic missions abroad and improvements in the speed and reliability of communications. The picture of a U.S. warship swinging at anchor, the commanding officer riding ashore in his gig in dress whites carrying a diplomatic dispatch to the chieftain of a remote republic, has changed over time only in the style of uniform and the lines of the ship, and not substantially in importance.

The U.S. Sixth Fleet during the late 1970s and 1980s was an essential instrument of the renowned but shaky U.S. foreign policy of "differentiation." In Ceausescu's oppressed Romania, regular port visits by U.S. warships allowed scores of American bluejackets ashore in dismal Black Sea ports to become the sole Western spectators of the most severely repressed outposts of the communist bloc.

Equally important was the Romanian contact with the American sailors. With Western tourism virtually nonexistent in Romania, the population had little other interface with citizens of the free world. In a society starved by its central authority of any knowledge of the outside world, this contact was crucial in keeping alive the spark of human hope. The juxtaposition of democracy with totalitarianism on the level of sailor with citizen is a largely overlooked phenomenon that scored well for the West. It surely kept the window of hope open for many citizens of a pathetic country where aspirations for a better life depended on such evidence that a better life existed at all.

Apart from the presence of Western diplomatic personnel and a handful of Western students, Romania was largely unvisited and, therefore, unknown to the free world until regular annual visits by U.S. warships began to the Black Sea port of Constanta in 1972. This was a period when, despite periodic thaws in superpower relations, there were no regular Western naval visits to the rest of the Soviet bloc. For that reason, both the U.S. Navy and the U.S. Embassy in Bucharest attached great importance to the annual summer visits to Constanta, which usually included a cruiser with eight hundred American sailors.

The Romanian Black Sea coast had sprouted a string of holiday resorts. They were constructed of immense and supremely ugly prefabricated concrete blocks formed into large complexes resembling shabby prisons. These resorts served as one of the few warm, seashore meccas for the Warsaw Pact party elite. The resorts, named after planets, accepted as guests only group tours from communist bloc countries.

The International Hotel in Constanta, however, was allowed to accept a few visiting Western vacationers. The International Hotel was heavily guarded by the Securitate to keep Romanians and other Eastern visitors away from the Western guests.

The brown dirt and sand beaches along this stretch of coastline were lined with bathers from the sun-starved Soviet Union and other Eastern European countries. Into this milieu, in the height of the tourist season each year, came hundreds of American sailors from the U.S. Sixth Fleet.

During one of these navy visits an entire orchestra led by the first violinist tried to defect to the American attaché in full view of the entire Romanian Navy hierarchy. This unnerving event occurred during an intermission in a concert at the Mufatlar State Winery for visiting American naval officers. A half dozen members of the orchestra gathered behind the violinist and confirmed their intention to seek political asylum with the U.S. Navy—not later, but before the concert ended. The American officer was able to postpone the discussion until after the concert and later convinced them that their chances would be best if they delayed their attempt to gain political asylum for several years.

U.S. diplomats lived in constant fear that an attempted defection might end the strained good will shown by both sides during the annual port visit events. During the ship's presence at the piers, Romanian security often intimidated the local population to frighten them away from prolonged contact with Western sailors.

When the ships opened for public visiting, hundreds of curious young Romanians filed aboard. During this rare contact between Americans and Romanians, the crew served hot dogs, popcorn, ice cream, and cookies. The Romanian Navy liaison officers stood nervously on the sidelines, fearing that something would go wrong during these public visits.

To deter fraternization, hundreds of Romanian Naval Academy cadets were planted in two long ranks stretching from the ship's quarterdeck brow to the port gates. The police then forced all civilians to pass through this gauntlet, after surrendering their personal identity papers, before touring the ship. Every effort was made by the Romanian authorities to frighten and intimidate the crowds without spoiling the event for the visiting Americans.

When visitors toured the ship, they were given a "Welcome Aboard" brochure. The Romanian liaison officers objected to these visitor handouts. They claimed the brochures contained vicious propaganda. One year the defense ministry demanded a chance to review the pamphlets in advance for clearance. U.S. diplomats produced one of the traditional pamphlets that was to be translated into the Romanian language and took it to the ministry of defense. The sinister Commander Padara-riu at the ministry's Defense Liaison Section pointed out the offensive words. The pamphlets read that the ships were a part of the U.S. Sixth Fleet, NATO's deterrent striking force in southern Europe. The Romanians preferred that visiting U.S. ships emphasize the bilateral relationship and not use the term "NATO." The Americans ignored their protests and gave out the pamphlets unchanged. The Romanians in turn confiscated them from the crowds as they left the ships.

It was always a relief to see the same number of visiting Romanians leave the ships as had boarded for the tours. For the average American sailor, most likely seeing control and repression for the first time in his life, the open display of cruelty toward the public by police and the military often fed an impulse to strike out subtly against what was observed. Sailors sometimes did this with a touch of genius.

Once, in the tense atmosphere following public visiting, the identity cards of two young Romanian girls remained unclaimed with the police after the crowds had left the ship. Terror shone in the eyes of the senior Romanian liaison officer, Commander Padarariu, as he confronted the U.S. attaché. "We must find those girls," he said almost pleading. "We must or there will never be another ship visit."

The U.S. Navy would not permit the Romanians to search the ships, which were sovereign American soil, but they were also keen not to let the incident get out of control. After a thorough but quiet check by the ship's company failed to find the girls, the day's activities continued. Shortly following the evening reception for the ship's company, hosted by the Romanian Navy, the two attractive Romanian girls appeared mysteriously on the arms of two American sailors strolling in a Constanta park. The Romanians were visibly relieved, but no one ever discovered how they had clandestinely departed from the ship.

A more vicious incident occurred in June 1984, when a group of Securitate thugs attacked five Americans, including three U.S. Embassy personnel, during a Navy port visit to Constanta. The Securitate used rubber truncheons and brass knuckles in the bloody fracas. Sadly, a broken bottle thrust by one Romanian into the face of one of the embassy marine security guards caused the loss of his eye.

As the naval liaison with the Romanians, the attaché was awakened at three that morning in a Constanta hotel and told by a frantic survivor of the brawl that the wounded marine had disappeared in a Securitate vehicle with one of the U.S. Embassy army personnel and was nowhere to be found.

Knowing the young marine had been injured, embassy officers began a systematic search of Constanta first aid stations and hospitals. Eventually, they came to an unbelievably deplorable hospital on an unlighted road. A sullen guard in a Securitate uniform summoned a frightened nurse who acknowledged that an American had been brought in earlier. The nurse escorted the officers into a dimly lit office that smelled of sweet disinfectant and urine. After a short wait, an

English-speaking doctor entered the room wearing a smock that had probably once been white but was now covered with both old, darkened blood stains and fresh, bright red stains.

The doctor spoke in a whisper and shook her head sadly, which led the diplomats instantly to fear that the marine had died. She led them into a room with ten beds. The walls were colored in two shades of what might have been green, but were smeared with stains. The ceiling was splattered with dark bloodstains, and several cockroaches scurried along the wall.

The Americans were taken to the bedside of a figure covered in dark blankets. A young man lay with his head wrapped in gray bandages covering both eyes. A dark stain was oozing from one eye. The poor marine was conscious and amazingly coherent, answering to his name. "I'm fine sir, just can't see through these bandages."

"I'm afraid I had to remove the left eye," the doctor whispered coldly in good English. "It came out in five lacerated pieces. Hopefully there was no damage to the optical nerve."

Assuring the marine he would be evacuated shortly, and leaving an embassy consular officer to stay with him, the diplomats quickly departed the dismal hospital, fighting the urge to vomit. They raced to the U.S. ships from which they ordered a military medical evacuation "Nightingale" flight from Rhein Main Air Base in Frankfurt, Germany.

The most unforgettable part of the entire episode was the reaction by the Romanians when the U.S. Air Force medical evacuation aircraft arrived at the Constanta airport several hours later. Two U.S. Embassy officers stood next to two Romanian officers and watched the glistening C-9 jet, with the American flag emblazoned on its tail, taxi toward them and stop on the tarmac a few yards from an ambulance holding the injured marine. A large door opened in the side of the aircraft and a platform slowly and smoothly descended as if by magic.

A Romanian standing with the Americans asked suddenly, "How many Americans are you evacuating?"

"One," they answered.

"Only one?" the officer asked, astounded. "You sent this huge airplane to pick up just one man?"

Three air force attendants, dressed in sparkling white, quickly wheeled the patient from the ambulance onto the platform that then ascended smoothly and disappeared into the fuselage. The aircraft began to taxi again as the large door closed and sealed. It was back in the air after spending less than ten minutes on the ground. The embassy officers walked away with the amazed Romanians, quietly thankful for being American.

Biblical Reflection

King Solomon built a fleet of ships at Ezion-geber, which is near Eloth on the shore of the Red Sea, in the land of Edom. Hiram sent his servants with the fleet, sailors who were familiar with the sea, together with the servants of Solomon. 1 Kings 9:26-27

Cultural exchanges made many Old Testament leaders extremely wary due to the fear that such exchanges might dilute their own religious practices and beliefs. Nevertheless, out of necessity, trade and state visits did occur with regularity. Even naval visits are recorded, as in the case of King Solomon's fleet of ships, built at Ezion-Geber and manned in part by Phoenician sailors under the orders of Hiram, king of Tyre.

First Kings 9:26-28 describes the routes and the purposes of these ship visits, and it also emphasizes the role of experienced seamen in carrying out the agreements between Solomon and Hiram. Apparently the cooperation between Israel and Tyre was successful, and the two kings were able to peacefully negotiate the occasional disputes recorded in the same chapter.

Envoy visits in the Old Testament did not always turn out well. Both King David and King Hezekiah encountered troubles as they dealt with other royal houses through emissaries. In one instance, David sent a delegation to express his sympathy at the death of King Nahash of the Ammonites. Unfortunately, Nahash's son Hanun, the newly crowned king, listened to his advisors, who were suspicious of David's gesture. They convinced Hanun that David's men had come to spy and explore their country in order to overthrow it. Though none of this was true, the king was swayed by his advisors and had his men humiliate members of David's delegation by shaving off their beards and cutting off their garments so that their buttocks were exposed!

These offenses were grave, but suspicion seemed to grip the Ammonites and they made the situation even worse by preparing for war. The war preparation included amassing many hired troops. This action was motivated by their fear that David would attack and not by any actual acts of aggression or threats from David himself. War did break out due to the Ammonites' failure to recognize the honorable nature of David's diplomatic overture.

David, though offended by the treatment of his ambassadors, counseled them to stay in Jericho until their beards grew back and then to come home. Of course, when he saw his neighbors amassing troops against him, he responded swiftly and decisively. Under the leadership of his very able army commander Joab, the Ammonites and their hired troops were thoroughly routed.

The entire engagement was the result of the harmful, insular vision of Hanun's advisors and their failure to receive the delegation from David with any sense of true diplomacy. In addition to being defeated by David's army, Hanun was defeated by the xenophobia of his own court.

A later king of Judah, Hezekiah, represents the opposite side of the coin. Though he had dealt reasonably with foreign diplomats in the past, in his later years he was so forthcoming with foreign visitors that he virtually invited the downfall of his own kingdom. When the king of Babylon sent a delegation bearing gifts to celebrate the recovery of Hezekiah from an illness, Hezekiah went to great lengths to show them every treasure in his kingdom. All of his wealth, his armory, his storehouses, and every feature of the realm were disclosed to the Babylonian envoys. The prophet Elijah was appalled at the extent of this indiscreet disclosure and rightly predicted that the Babylonians would someday be back to sack the kingdom.

There are often risks to legitimate self-interests—but also very real chances for mutual benefit—when nations attempt to engage each other. Where is the balance between a people protecting their own interests while at the same time being open to learning and benefiting from other sovereign peoples? The answer lies in laws and protocols that enable honorable interactions to occur.

One well-known example is the successful state visit to King Solomon by the Queen of Sheba, who wanted to see for herself some of the innovations she had heard about under Solomon's kingship. She arrived with ceremony and with a spectacularly large entourage. She, Solomon, and their people on each side apparently behaved with courtesy and the proprieties that each monarch could rightfully expect of the other. The implications in Scripture are that gifts were exchanged, meals shared, and deep conversations about justice and righteousness took place, along with the opportunity to visit and observe as was appropriate.

In their honorable treatment of each other, a friendship developed between Solomon and the queen. Interestingly, though it was the queen who was on a fact-finding mission, Solomon was introduced to new commercial products and received more wealth to the benefit of his kingdom. The African queen had brought with her huge quantities of rare spices and other items unknown to Solomon. When she returned with her retinue to her own country, she departed in peace.

One of the things that the Queen of Sheba had particularly noted was how happy the people of the land must be given the ideas of justice and righteousness she and Solomon had discussed. Perhaps even more than the talk, she was struck by how he treated his trusted cupbearers, his officials, and his other servants. His actions were his witness.

Some people who are not particularly religious wince at the use of the word *righteousness*, but righteousness, the path of seeking out and doing right things, is the fundamental basis for all fair laws. Justice and righteousness go hand in hand.

In contemporary societies, words of agreement remain important; courtesy, diplomacy, and integrity in honoring agreements remain essential. Still, a louder and more compelling witness than words is found in the treatment of individuals—whether cupbearer or wounded soldier—by those in authority. The Romanian incident is a case in point. In an atmosphere where just one matters, the ideas of justice and righteousness take on added power.

CHAPTER 16

The Old Croat

nte looked every part the hero he was, despite his seventy-odd years. He was tall and lean and conveyed the air of someone with complete confidence without being pompous. When he looked at you he had a way of implying that he shared a secret with you. He seemed always trying to catch you in the act of beginning to smile and had a way of sneaking up on your thoughts. We often sat for long periods of silence looking out from his covered garden on the island of Korchula—just thinking together.

Ante loved the sea and was possessive of everything it offered. As a war hero he was allowed the privilege of using a fish trap in violation of local law. He ate only fish and fruit. He drank only wine and *loza*, the distilled grape liquor, for they were close to the land.

Ante Milina, *nom de guerre* "Pershona," was the World War II hero of Korchula. He had led more by his strength of character than by assigned rank or position within Tito's Partisan organization. He led his guerillas in the fight to defend Korchula from the Germans and he would do that again against anyone else who harmed or threatened the people of that island pearl in the Adriatic. In fact, Ante's force had made excursions to Korchula so costly for the Germans that they generally gave it a wide berth and, except for one serious attempt to pacify it, they mostly gave it up.

One of more than fourteen hundred islands sprinkled along the Dalmatian coast, Korchula boasted its own walled city, rivaling Dubrovnik in beauty if not size. The island was built by Venetians and had changed hands often during Roman times. Like Dubrovnik, Korchula had been an independent republic with a long history of producing mariners. Marco Polo was among the many famous sailors born in the walled city; his grave still stand above the ancient town of Orebić on the tip of Peljeshac Peninsula. The peninsula juts out from the dry coastline on a northwesterly stance midway between the coastal towns of Split to the north and Dubrovnik to the south. Nearby is the mouth of the Neretva River, which flows into the rich plain near Ploche after tumbling down through the heights of Bosnia, past Sarajevo and Mostar, and finally empties majestically into the Adriatic.

Ante was widely known along the coast. Tito awarded him two homes for his bravery in the fight against the Germans. One home was in Gruz, the port of Dubrovnik, and the other was a comfortable villa on the far side of Korchula, not far from Smokvica, a vineyard renowned for its smoky white wine.

One of the more significant privileges Ante enjoyed as a result of his status as Partisan hero was the regular delivery by barge of the precious commodity of water. Most of the numerous Dalmatian islands were without natural ground water and, except where the Neretva River emptied its valuable cool waters from the Sarajevo/Mostar Pass, there was little natural water available anywhere on that barren coast. For this reason, the entire coastal area was dry and parched for much of the year and littered with unproductive vineyards and olive groves. These had prospered during the years when the land had been painstakingly irrigated by hand and sweat of brow. However, there had been a great blight on the grapes before the war and the local population failed to begin cultivation again after the war. The personal incentives fostered by private ownership, which, in the past, had driven the locals to till and irrigate the vineyards and olive groves, were gone under the communist system. The Dalmatian region of the

Croatian Republic became a barren land, the Mediterranean climate and lifestyle good only for attracting tourists from Europe.

After World War II, the coastline erupted with ugly tourist enclaves gouged out of the serene cliffs overlooking the Adriatic. Although natural sandy beaches were rare, the enclaves cleverly made the coast attractive for swimmers by constructing stone platforms that abutted the clear seas for swimmers and sunbathers.

The more opulent of these complexes were built for wealthy Western tourists, largely Germans and British. These were interspersed among more austere, larger, and sterile-looking resort hotel complexes designed for large tour groups from Eastern European countries, whose people generally lacked the freedom of individual holiday travel. Thus the very popular Adriatic coast became a mecca for both East and West. Of course, the clever Dalmatian hosts did their best to keep tourists from East and West completely separated from each other.

Ante Milina lived from the sea and by the sea. He would never harm a soul who didn't interfere with his peaceful life on Korchula. He rarely visited his Dubrovnik home in the summer season since the city was then too crowded for his liking. In the winter, especially when the strong, northerly storm winds called *bura* blew, he liked to be in Dubrovnik. His winter house looked to the north directly in the path of the wind-churned seas. After the *bura* there would be cold clear weather that Ante said inspired everyone to great deeds. Apart from the winter *bura* cycles, Ante preferred the isolation of Korchula.

Ante refused to accept the notion that communist ideals drove his Partisan units during the war. He believed that the only issue at hand during his heroic stand against the Germans was the defense of his island against an invader. He said he would fight again to protect his lands. But he never got that chance. After the Croatian secession bid in 1991, the

Yugoslav Navy, run mostly by Serbs, went about conducting random, vengeful raids along the Croatian coast, killing for no good reason in an attempt to racially cleanse Yugoslavia of all Croats. Ante was killed in 1992 in a naval bombardment of Dubrovnik conducted just for spite.

Biblical Reflection

The LORD does not see as mortals see; they look on the outward appearance, but the LORD looks on the heart. I Samuel 16:7b

Pershona was not individually targeted, and his killing was in some sense impersonal; nevertheless, it was the direct result of hatred. At first glance, hatred seems to be entirely negative. Realistically, however, the capacity to hate is a part of our ability to discern and choose between what is good and what is not. Seen this way, hatred as a human response is not without good purpose. There are things, ideas, and situations we should rightfully hate and reject; however, the blind, undiscriminating hatred of persons as individuals or as groups warrants close examination.

Pershona was part of a group that was completely expendable according to those firing weapons toward Dubrovnik. Is such hatred ever to be understood and tolerated?

The hatred of persons is a peculiar and pervasive thing. It never arises out of righteous cooperation among people, but out of sin. To be fair, the sin underlying hatred does not have to originate within the people who hate. Actions against us can cause us to hate. Consider, for instance, hatred toward murderers, rapists, and others who rob us of our loved ones and our peace and security. It is said that we should hate the sin and not the sinner, but that is an argument for another day.

It remains the case that sinful acts—our own or those of others—can draw us into the realm of hating others. It is also the case that sin and hate combined have destructive consequences for all. Many suffer as a result of hatred. So how do we get a grip on hate and put it in its proper place? What do we do in the face of hatred on such a grand scale that it promotes and justifies reprehensible ideas like the ethnic cleansing that took Pershona's life?

Though the particular phrase *ethnic cleansing* came into use in the twentieth century, many accounts exist in the Bible of one population attempting to wipe out an entire population of others, showing no mercy for anyone. Examples from the Old Testament include the intended destruction of the Canaanites, as related in Deuteronomy, where not even the animals were to be left alive when Joshua led his forces through the promised land. Scorched-earth practices were not isolated or unique events, and people we consider heroes participated. Conquered people, already defeated militarily, often met terrible fates at the hands of the winners.

To add to the burden of our history, ethnic division and intolerance is by no means limited to Old Testament texts. The animosities between Jews and Samaritans, as well as between Romans and conquered peoples, are rather matter-of-factly acknowledged in the New Testament. One troubling and unexpected example of this in the New Testament is the encounter between Jesus and a Gentile woman recorded in the Gospels of Mark and Matthew.

Jesus himself seems to affirm the low regard with which Jews looked at Gentiles. Indeed, until one reads the entire passage, Jesus seems to be as much a racist, classist, or sexist as anyone else in his day and culture. The encounter is described in both Mark 7:24-30 and Matthew 15:21-28. Here is Matthew's account.

> Jesus left that place and went away to the district of Tyre and Sidon. Just then a Canaanite woman from that region came out and started shouting, "Have mercy on me, Lord, Son of David; my daughter is tormented by a demon." But he did not answer her at all. And his disciples came and

urged him, saying, "Send her away, for she keeps shouting after us." He answered, "I was sent only to the lost sheep of the house of Israel." But she came and knelt before him, saying, "Lord, help me." He answered, "It is not fair to take the children's food and throw it to the dogs." She said, "Yes, Lord, yet even the dogs eat the crumbs that fall from their masters' table." Then Jesus answered her, "Woman, great is your faith! Let it be done for you as you wish." And her daughter was healed instantly.

Since this is the same Jesus who challenges us to be new beings, I think we can assume that a conventional understanding of this story simply won't do. We have here a teaching moment by the one who often declared, "You have heard it said . . . but I say unto you . . ." as he invested ancient beliefs with new meaning.

The disciples who witnessed this strange encounter between Jesus and a Gentile woman would have been steeped in the cultural belief that some people could be rightfully regarded as mere dogs simply because of their ethnicity. They tried to send her away and they certainly would not have been aghast at anyone from their circle using such language as Jesus did with the Gentile woman. Who was she, after all? A *Gentile* and a *woman*! But on that day, she was also their object lesson.

The Gentile woman knew well that the gathered disciples might esteem her little, but she was willing to risk rejection in the power of her love for her little daughter. She had strong hopes and aspirations for their lives together and she was willing to take extreme measures to get a blessing for the both of them. And so she approached Jesus to beg him to heal her daughter. She was willing to come forward and impress upon Jesus in whatever way necessary that she was a woman aching for a blessing from God just as any other person created in the image of God might seek such a blessing.

Whether the disciples recognized in her someone of stature or not, she recognized herself to be a person both longing for and deserving of grace. Jesus knew these things about her. Jesus shattered the wall of prejudice between people by granting her the blessing for which she asked. She did not have to become someone "special." She was special.

The disciples could not have been left unchanged by this encounter. At first they had heard Jesus apparently confirming their prejudice and no doubt they smiled smugly. And then the master teacher confounded their arrogance by granting the woman what she had asked for—her daughter was healed, her faith was praised.

The Gentile woman stands as a metaphor for how the outsider is so often viewed. She stands for all the rejected. Are persons dogs? The truth is not even dogs are "dogs" in God's creation. When dogs are recognized as magnificent creatures with astounding capacities—and treated as such— humans reap marvelous companionship and amazing help from these creatures. How much more do we all benefit when all people are recognized as members of a human community who deserve to enjoy God's gifts in an atmosphere of peace, justice, wholeness, and harmony? The tensions and conflicts we experience in life are based on real issues and require real answers, but can hatred of one another and deadly violence be our only choices when confronting those issues?

Ironically and sadly, sometimes war has been necessary to defend and protect the vulnerable and to preserve that which allows justice to flourish in the face of unbridled hatred. In a world where for millennia wars of aggression and exploitation have been sanctioned by religion and at times even fought under the banner of religion, the task before us is to keep hatred in its proper place. Hatred must not be used as a rationale for greed and aggression or to justify deaths such as Pershona's. We are called on to hate the things that destroy community and that are counter to living out God's purposes. We will likely continue to fight one another in this world. Fighting rages across the globe even as I write these words.

Though we are called to accord, there is no such accord—but there is light and we should not despair. The light shines in Christ's call to shun evil and do good, and to seek peace among ourselves, a theme that permeates all Scripture. One day, it will be as Isaiah proclaimed:

> They shall beat their swords into plowshares,
> and their spears into pruning hooks;
> nation shall not lift up sword against nation,
> neither shall they learn war any more. Isaiah 2:4

The active pursuit of peace, the active pursuit of justice, the active departing from evil are not easy, but they are necessary if we are to limit the fruits of hate and begin to allow the light of Christ to penetrate our darkness. Mine is not a pacifist position, nor am I engaging in anti-military rhetoric. The active pursuit of peace and justice does require teeth to enforce such ideals, but the morality guiding the employment of military force is what makes the difference between just and unjust use of that force, and determines whether human beings can achieve security and realize the hope for closer community. It is imperative that the ideals of peace never be discounted and that Isaiah's vision never be considered unattainable. The energies of war must serve this vision, not replace the vision.

CHAPTER 17

My Brush with History

I n late May 1988, the atmosphere in Moscow was heady with the advent of the Gorbachev-Reagan summit. In the U.S. Embassy we were repeatedly surprised by the abrupt disappearance of the usual bureaucratic obfuscation that accompanied diplomatic planning in the Soviet capital. A rare experience of eager cooperation appeared magically at every step leading toward the presidential meeting.

The day of the summit arrived, and with it planeloads of American officials and the press descending on a polished Moscow determined to present its best face. Winter residue had disappeared, buildings were freshly painted, and even public transport wore a bright new look. Flowers appeared miraculously in full bloom and clear, warm weather burst over a capital notorious for its gray funk.

Secretary of Defense Frank Carlucci arrived ahead of the presidential party to meet with Soviet Defense Minister Dmitry Yazov to begin substantive talks that eventually led to the successful Intermediate-range Nuclear Forces Treaty and ultimately to further breakthroughs in arms control. Carlucci was an avid long-distance swimmer and wished to start his Moscow days early with a brisk mile in the embassy pool. As the embassy's naval attaché, I was customarily accorded all water-related tasks, and thus I was assigned to escort the secretary during his daily swim.

At 6:00 A.M. on the first day of the defense meetings, we plunged into the embassy pool and my breathless half-mile barely matched Carlucci's time for a full mile. While alone in the locker room after the swim, we discussed the prospects for the formal talks that were to open at the Soviet Ministry of Defense later that morning. Carlucci was cautiously optimistic.

President Gorbachev had announced a deadline for Soviet military withdrawal from Afghanistan, so there remained only one hurdle for the start of meaningful military negotiations: U.S. insistence on a Soviet apology for the heinous killing three years earlier of U.S. Army Major Arthur D. Nicholson Jr. of the U.S. Military Liaison Mission in East Germany.

Carlucci asked, "You know the Soviet military, what are the chances we'll get an apology for the Nicholson killing today?"

After some reflection, I replied that, judging from the surprisingly cordial conduct of the Soviets during the pre-summit preparations, I thought he would receive the apology.

Later that day I stood in uniform in the ornate Soviet Defense Ministry conference room waiting the arrival of the Carlucci party. As embassy site-control officer for the defense talks, I was assigned to ensure a telephone line was available at all times for the secretary of defense to talk across Moscow with President Reagan should the need arise. Relations between the United States and the Soviet Union had not yet improved sufficiently to trust a secure scrambler telephone in the Soviet defense sanctum.

I waited by the designated telephone with my counterpart, a nervous-looking Soviet Army colonel, and watched the Carlucci party approach. The gaggle of senior officials walked briskly down the ornate hallway under overpowering murals painted in the style of socialist realism. The murals screamed from the walls to remind all who passed of the Nazi defeat on the eastern front, the sole positive achievement of seventy years of communism. All visiting delegations were subjected to the garish forms painted on the walls and ceiling, heroes of the Great Patriotic War peering down like cherubs along the wide corridor to the imposing doors of the minister's conference room.

The talks began and, after several moments of delicate fencing by both sides, the shrill ring of the special phone suddenly silenced the room. My Soviet counterpart froze when all at the conference table turned abruptly toward the two of us. The colonel's eyes locked in panic. A tense pause followed. Seeing he was not going to pick up the phone as planned, I took the receiver and in my best Russian answered, "Good morning, this is the Soviet Ministry of Defense, Captain Huchthausen, United States Navy, speaking."

The unidentified caller froze in disbelief at my answer, and then swore richly in Russian, "They've overrun the ministry!"

When the talks adjourned for the day, the hosts escorted the Americans back into the long high-ceilinged corridor. The corpulent Marshal Yazov took the slender Carlucci brusquely by the arm and steered him into a large adjoining office. The only other person allowed into the room with the two powerful defense ministers was Carlucci's interpreter, a young American woman. The doors closed and a pause of several minutes followed while the remaining officers from both sides waited nervously in the corridor. The doors opened abruptly and the two ministers emerged looking solemn as they filed silently out and down the stairs, followed by the throng of generals and admirals.

Early the next morning after our swim, Secretary Carlucci said, "Captain, you were right, I got an apology."

On June 2, their last day in Moscow, President and Mrs. Reagan rode in a motorcade past crowds of curious but smiling Muscovites to Vnukovo Airport and departure. Feeling greatly relieved, I stood in the line of U.S. Embassy officers arranged for the airport farewell. Following elaborate Soviet military honors, President Reagan passed slowly down the rank of U.S. diplomats saying a few words to each. As he stepped in front of me, I groped for appropriate words. "Mr.

President," I stammered, "I never thought I'd meet you for the first time here in the Soviet Union."

Without missing a beat the president replied, "And I never thought I'd meet you here either, captain!" and threw back his head and laughed with typical Reagan warmth. The rest is history.

Biblical Reflection

A soft answer turns away wrath. Proverbs 15:1

On one of his many military campaigns, David needed to replenish food supplies for his troops and, as was the custom of the time, he sent word to a rich landholder named Nabal asking for provisions. Nabal (whose name means "fool") was churlish and unreasonable, and refused. Not only did he refuse, he also insulted David personally by implying that David was a nobody of questionable background.

David's men returned to him empty handed and made their report. Naturally, the young king was stirred to anger and determined to show Nabal exactly whom he had offended. David strapped on his weapons and ordered four hundred of his men to take up their swords and follow him while the rest stayed behind to guard the camp.

All would have been lost for Nabal if others had not intervened. A young worker had overheard the exchange between David's men and Nabal. He reported the incident to Abigail, Nabal's wife. He told Abigail that prior to the encounter where Nabal insulted David, David's men had treated everyone on their land very well. The young worker, knowing his master's ill temper, had thought it best to let Abigail know what had transpired. He rightfully assumed there would be retaliation.

Without informing her husband, Abigail elected to try to make amends and so turn aside the disaster heading their way. She hurriedly gathered two hundred loaves of bread, skins of wine, some dressed sheep, grains, raisins, and figs, and loaded these provisions on animals to supply David's men.

It was David's stated intention to kill every male who belonged to the place. He felt justified in this because he had guarded Nabal's estate and had seen to it that his men in no way abused anything that belonged to Nabal. The insult he received in return was inexcusable in that day.

Abigail met David as he came up the mountain toward her home. She alighted from her donkey, and her deferential behavior and eloquent words demonstrated how deeply sorry she was for the offense of her household. She asked David to consider her alone guilty, and she begged of him to take the food offerings and to believe in the sincerity of her apology.

David was so moved by Abigail's actions that he turned from his intention to do harm. He assured her that, had she not come to meet him as she did, not one male would have been alive in Nabal's household the next morning. He let Abigail go in peace, again telling her that her voice had reached him.

The impolitic, foolish, and wrong actions of others can create a miasma of additional harmful problems. The failure to make amends is tantamount to literally adding insult to injury. Demanding acknowledgement of, and an apology for, the wrongful death of Major Nicholson was equivalent to allowing someone to speak on behalf the Soviet Nabals who caused his death. The Soviet defense minister did just that. The apology needed to occur for any other concerns to be addressed in a sincere way.

No one can say with certainty how the Gorbachev-Reagan summit would have concluded if the Soviets had not offered an apology to Secretary Carlucci, but it is certain that the extension of an apology provided an additional glimmer of light as the talks proceeded.

CHAPTER 18

The Last Comrade

The dramatic collapse of the Berlin Wall was echoed in the Moscow diplomatic community by the reactions of our colleagues, the military and naval attachés from Eastern European capitals. During the previous two-and-one-half years, I had developed a close personal friendship with East German naval attaché Captain Rolf Franke.

Rolf was the senior naval officer in the embassy of the German Democratic Republic (GDR). He had served as an intelligence officer his entire career and probably hadn't seen a ship or the sea since he was a naval cadet in Berlin. He had served as an attaché and advisor in Cuba, Peru, Vietnam, and in several other overseas assignments he preferred not to mention.

As with most Warsaw Pact attachés serving outside their native countries, he was permitted to take only his wife to his country of assignment. For purported reasons of schooling, the Eastern attachés were required to leave children (or one other family member) behind, especially when they served in the West. Some called it ransom; others called it insurance that they would return home.

Rolf had grandchildren who visited on occasion from Berlin. His wife, Jutta, grew more somber and morose the longer she lived in Moscow and the more the situation in her native East Germany deteriorated. Rolf invited me frequently to his embassy, located nearby on Leninskiy Prospect, and he became more outspoken as the situation in Berlin changed.

Rolf began to speak openly with me about his retirement plans, his salary, and the situation at home. He professed to be a devout communist, but admitted that their system had been making grave errors for years. He was openly critical of East German President Hoenecker when we were alone. Had the times been normal, I would have categorized him as a perfect example of an official preparing to defect. But if that was his intention it was overtaken completely by the rapidly unfolding events in Berlin. As it turned out, Rolf's entire homeland defected to the West before he could.

Rolf confided that he feared for his safety and that of his family. When the news broke about the sacking of the East German Security Police (STASI) headquarters in Berlin, Rolf was in my home visiting. He told me he planned to bring his entire family to Moscow until the situation was clarified. Rolf explained to me that his career record would certainly preclude a normal retirement, and he might even be jailed if he went back. It was truly a sorrowful experience for him.

The leaders of the communist East deserve no pity for their fate and are rightly held accountable for policies that resulted in the many tragic deaths of citizens who tried to escape those policies. The broken homes and the physical and mental suffering of their populace stand as witnesses against them. Nevertheless, many Western diplomats serving in the East truly felt pity for Warsaw Pact military officers like Rolf, whose lives unraveled during that period.

The denouement of the East/West military relationship came during the 1989 annual East German Armed Forces Day celebration. That year was the fortieth anniversary of the German Democratic Republic and the founding of their armed forces. A grand diplomatic event was scheduled just one month before the Berlin Wall crumbled and the future of Germany rested on the whims of Soviet General Secretary Gorbachev and the Politburo. The GDR anniversary became more than just a national day; it was the last great fling in Moscow staged by any Warsaw Pact military organization.

I went in my dress blues to the contemporary GDR Embassy chancery, which, although built in a radical, *avant-garde* architectural style, was not totally unattractive in the usual sense of communist architecture. The main reception hall held three huge crystal chandeliers resembling something out of King Ludwig's fantasy castles in Bavaria. Walls of white marble lined the entrance and staircase.

The event was spectacular. Many East German military officers were present in their dress uniforms, along with scores of both senior and ancient Soviet generals and admirals. Many of these were retired senior officers who had served a good deal of their post-war careers inside Germany, where the cream of the Soviet Army was stationed.

An unexpectedly large number of young East German officers attended, having converged on Moscow from the many military training establishments around the Soviet Union, where officers from all the Warsaw Pact armies studied. There were more than four hundred student officers from the GDR, most of them young lieutenants and captains, attending Soviet combat arms schools. The more senior field grade officers attended the Voroshilov General Staff Academy. They looked like modern Wehrmacht officers, arrayed as they were in their gray-and-silver dress uniforms with old World War II insignia and high polished boots.

The tables lining the hall were bedecked with food: Russian caviar, sturgeon, sliced tongue, mushrooms with sour cream, dark breads, German sausage, salami, potato salads, and pickled herring of every color and description. Chilled bottles of Russian vodka and champagne interspersed with bottles of German schnapps and beer accompanied the food. In addition, small kegs of East German pilsner beer stood in every corner. A bevy of young pink-cheeked Russian and German waitresses in tight black dresses, white blouses with starched aprons, and white tiaras fluttered among the uniforms.

The East German ambassador, resplendent in full diplomat uniform with brightly colored medals and sash, greeted the guests at the head of a receiving line. The East German attaché contingent of twelve officers in full dress uniforms stood by the ambassador, resembling a scene from Tolstoy's *War and Peace*. My friend Rolf stood at his spot in the line, several down from the major general defense attaché, who looked as if he were about to explode with emotion.

I was astounded to see the number of senior Soviets in attendance. The Soviet deputy ministers of defense and chiefs of each service were there. I had never before seen the entire Soviet naval hierarchy together in one room at the same time. Soviet Defense Minister Yazov arrived accompanied by the chief of the general staff, General of the Army Moiseev.

Rolf later joined me when the receiving line had trickled to a small contingent. The noise level was impressive. There was a short welcome address by the GDR ambassador and then the toasts began. Given the slightest excuse, the Russians are great toasters. Beginning with Minister Yazov and proceeding down the line, Soviet and East German officers, active and retired, stepped up one by one to a microphone and gave toast after toast—flowery, verbose, patriotic, and morbid. The process continued for more than an hour. The later it grew the longer and less articulate the toasts.

Rolf took me by the arm and guided me through the throng to a short man in an East German Navy uniform. He introduced me in the din to the chief of the East German Navy, a vice admiral I first met in May 1988, at the bier of Admiral of the Fleet of the Soviet Union Gorshkov, founder of the modern Soviet Navy. When I reminded him of our first meeting, the admiral smiled wanly and said, "Ah, we meet again, at another wake."

We encountered Soviet Navy commander in chief Admiral Vladimir Chernavin trying to converse with a circle of military attachés through a German interpreter who was having difficulty speaking. The situation worsened when, in the course of another toast drunk from tall tumblers, the poor interpreter finished his glass, staggered forward, and fell in a heap like a rag doll. Those around pretended it hadn't happened.

At the microphone a senior German general gave a long toast into which a number of old and corpulent Russian generals joined in. I gathered from the toast that it was to old comrades who had served together on the front and who were now watching the collapse of the alliance without a shot fired.

A deep baritone voice began singing the "Internationale" and the entire room joined in. Dramatically, the officer giving the toast emptied his glass and flung it across the room at a marble wall, where it splintered. That triggered a barrage of glasses launched against the wall. The singing continued. Out of the corner of my eye I saw another uniform crumple on the floor and still another limp German being carried out feet first.

Rolf pulled me to the side as we watched food and glasses flying through the air. The singing and toasting continued and Rolf finally guided me to a side room where we sat in large easy chairs and talked over coffee and cognac. The sound in the main room grew dimmer. We talked for a long time until Rolf drifted off, his head lolling on his chest. It was after midnight when I rose and made my way quietly toward the main staircase, past the entrance to the main hall and the still-glowing chandeliers.

I glanced inside as I passed the grand hall—it was a shambles. Bottles and broken glass were scattered on the floor; food littered the large tables. I continued down the ornate staircase past the large picture of Lenin looking down into the cavernous, empty entrance. Lenin was bracketed on each side by red, black, and gold flags and above by the large crest of the German Democratic Republic, a gilded hammer and compass surrounded by a wreath of golden grain.

I entered the dark cloakroom, my eyes not yet accustomed to the shadows. After groping a while in the dark, I found my navy bridge coat hanging on the long coat rack, took it down, and while struggling with its torn lining, saw sudden movement toward the back of the room. Several German officer great coats were lying on the floor, embroidered silver insignia glittering in the dim light. As I moved toward the sound, expecting to encounter another victim of the evening's repeated toasts, I nearly tripped on a writhing mass partially hidden in the darkness. I bent over to see what was there, and suddenly made out the form of a German officer with his uniform tunic open and with no trousers, sprawled on a pile of coats, copulating furiously with a partially-nude Russian waitress, black dress above her naked waist.

I stepped out into the cold night and into snowflakes blowing nearly horizontally. A solitary German guard saluted by the entrance as I walked toward the parking lot. Hours earlier when I arrived, the large area had been full of sleek black Chaika and Zil limousines delivering senior Soviet military officers. The lot was now empty except for one black Chaika with the engine running, the driver asleep behind the wheel in the warm interior. I walked across the parking block past a spot where snow clearly showed the imprint of a large car, long departed, and stepped over a crumpled Soviet senior officer's winter fur *shapka* lying in the snow, covered with vomit, slowly being re-covered with new snow.

Walking through the cold Moscow night toward the lights of Lenin Prospect, dim in the snowfall, the brass-band tones of the "Internationale" still echoed in my ears. The scene I had just witnessed was the last act in a bad play starring the Warsaw Pact military. The end was at hand. I had just witnessed the second playing of the Gotterdammerung. One month and two days later, at 3:30 P.M. on November 9, following Gorbachev's appeal to open the borders to avoid an explosion, the Berlin Wall was breached and eventually destroyed.

Biblical Reflection

*Then the L*ORD *answered me and said:*
Write the vision;
make it plain on tablets,
so that a runner may read it.
For there is still a vision for the appointed time;
it speaks of the end, and does not lie.
If it seems to tarry, wait for it;
it will surely come, it will not delay.
Look at the proud!
Their spirit is not right in them,
but the righteous live by their faith. Habakkuk 2:2-4

In the Old Testament, the book of Habakkuk stands out as a critical social and political analysis and protest. It also stands as a beacon pointing toward the incorporation of justice and human dignity in the laws that govern societies. It is the prophet Habakkuk who declares that the righteous shall live by faith, and it is he who complains loudly to God in very specific terms about the wrongs that plagued his times—wrongs that continue to plague humanity.

It is to Habakkuk that God declares that woe will come to those who build their towns with blood and who found their cities on iniquity. It is inevitable that the day will come when those who are oppressed will awaken, rise up, and make the unrighteous tremble. These words of prophecy may seem old-fashioned, but they are words that continue to speak to conditions in the modern world.

The book of Habakkuk begins with the prophet questioning God:

How long, O LORD, must I call for help,
but you do not listen?
Or cry out to you, "Violence!"

but you do not save?
Why do you make me look at injustice?
Why do you tolerate wrong?
Destruction and violence are before me;
there is strife, and conflict abounds.
Therefore the law is paralyzed,
and justice never prevails.
The wicked hem in the righteous,
so that justice is perverted. Habakkuk 1:2-4 NIV

Habakkuk's complaints speak to the experiences of people who lived behind the iron curtain. People were literally hemmed in, unable to escape injustice, violence, conflict, strife, and the perversion of values associated with basic human rights. Bolshevik communism entirely fit the model indicted by Habakkuk in his analysis of power gone awry. Paralleling the biblical poetry, under communism a ruthless and impetuous people seized power, dwelled in places not their own, were a law unto themselves, promoted their own honor, gathered prisoners like sand, swept past like the wind—guilty men, whose own strength was their god. They were a dreaded and feared people who swept down like vultures to devour, but finally, as the prophet wrote, ruin came to those guilty of seizing things not their own.

As in "The Last Comrade," Habakkuk observed that the oppressors of his day seemed to enjoy the choicest food, to live in luxury, to swallow up the righteous. The oppressors piled up stolen goods, made themselves wealthy by extortion, made captives of all people, and gathered to them all the nations they could. But, Habakkuk declared, "the righteous live by their faith" (Habakkuk 2:4). What can this possibly mean?

Under Soviet oppression, many, in fact, did not live. Millions under Soviet rule were lost in the Gulags and to the machinations of cruel government programs of extermination and exploitation.

How do the righteous live by their faith and, indeed, what is the answer to Habakkuk's first searching question, "How long, O LORD?" This is a pivotal question that people living under oppression must always ask and answer in order to inspire action. Living by faith, especially in times of extreme circumstances, is what human beings do. To live in faith is to go on in hope that relief will come and justice will reign. We go on in the hope of survival and the hope of change. We go on in the hope of intervention and help. From where does the help come, and for how long must we wait? How will our hopes be justified?

Psalm 121 declares, "I lift my eyes to the hills—from where does my help come? My help comes from the LORD, who made heaven and earth," and Psalm 133:1 announces, "How very good and pleasant it is when kindred live together in unity!" Human beings find their strength in righteous community. When men and women live together in peace and unity, granting each other dignity and the respect due the children of God, humanity experiences the help of God. What is required is that we strive together for righteousness as communities. How long must we wait? We wait until the righteous have the courage and vision to rise up and demand righteousness—and fight for it.

The people at the reception in "The Last Comrade" are not essential to the story; they are not the ones who make the walls crumble. The oppressed, even the dead who live only in the memories of those left behind, are the important ones—those who finally stood together and said, "Enough!" Those who stood together recognizing and demanding their birthright as human beings are the ones who brought about the collapse of the wall. The force of righteousness can supply the fuel of wrath necessary to topple wrong and can empower people to do whatever is necessary to right wrongs.

Habakkuk's question, "What use is an idol once its maker has shaped it—a metal cast, a teacher of lies?" (2:18) can be rephrased as, "What use is a gilded hammer and compass surrounded by a wreath of gold, or the painted eyes of Lenin staring from a portrait?"

In 1 Corinthians 6:19, Paul asks: "Do you not know that your body is a temple of the Holy Spirit within you, which you have from God?" Habakkuk's confession that, "The LORD is in his holy temple; let all the earth keep silence before him!"(2:20) resounds within all humanity. The walls will crumble, the idols will topple, and the righteous will prevail because the purposes of God shine brighter than the greed and ambition of tyrants. Still, it is up to those who live by their faith to stand up in unity against evil, in whatever numbers we must. By standing as one, standing together, fighting the wrong, the light of our faith defeats the oppressor.

CHAPTER 19

Red Star Scuttled

B y the early autumn of 1989, Americans in Moscow were used to bizarre and unusual events. Since the summer of 1987, we had witnessed the INF Treaty breakthrough, the Reagan-Gorbachev summit, the Marshal Akhromeyev-Admiral Crowe exchanges, the consummation of the agreement for joint U.S./U.S.S.R. military cooperation, and the resumption of warship exchange visits. The Soviet Army was out of Afghanistan and Defense Minister Dmitry Yazov had apologized for the killing of Army Major Nicholson, shot by a Soviet sentry while working with the U.S. Military Liaison Mission in Berlin. It was hard to surprise anyone in the U.S. Embassy in Moscow in 1989.

I had just returned from another precedent-setting event, escorting the chief of naval operations, Admiral Carlisle Trost, and his delegation on a tour of key naval sites in the Soviet Union. He was the first of the U.S. military service chiefs to visit under the new agreement.

The news of growing unrest among Eastern European populations and the flaunting of their central authorities was broadcast daily on the Moscow evening television program, *Vremya*. More and more real life was being shown to the public, with *glasnost*—the recent Soviet policy of discussing social problems and shortcomings with refreshing candor—in its fourth year.

That October, the blatant confrontations between the people and the communist authorities in Hungary, Czechoslovakia, and East Germany were reported in surprising detail on the Moscow news. Those events, and the release of control of the Russian Orthodox Church, were building to a whirling crescendo. On Christmas Day 1989, the state evening television news showed the bullet-ridden bodies of Nicolai and Elena Ceausescu lying in the Romanian courtyard at Tirgoviste. That harrowing event, seen on every television in every home in the U.S.S.R., became a dark omen looming over the Moscow communist leadership until two years later when the hammer and sickle came tumbling down from the Kremlin to be replaced by the ancient Russian tri-color.

Biblical Reflection

The LORD watches over the way of the righteous, but the way of the wicked will perish. Psalm 1:6

Whether or not one is a biblical literalist, the sacred texts describing symbolic or historical events provide much food for thought when considering situations in modern times. One need only think of the televised bodies of the Ceausescus, which evoked well-founded fear in the minds of other communist leaders. While no viewer could forecast the precise results, the images of the fallen leaders certainly meant that further radical changes were in store.

A similar story in the apocalyptic book of Daniel recounts the strange downfall of Belshazzar, the son who succeeded Nebuchadnezzar as king of Babylon. During a night of revelry, Belshazzar ordered that all the gold and silver vessels looted from the temple in Jerusalem be brought to the feast, where he and his wives and concubines drank from them. He then proceeded to praise the gods of gold, silver, iron, bronze, wood, and stone much as the modern dictator Ceausescu enjoyed material excesses while mocking the labors of ordinary Romanians.

The harsh and costly deprivations Ceausescu imposed on Romanian citizens while he and his family lived in luxury mirrors Belshazzar's mockery. Rather than being the heroic leader he might have been, in view of some of his early reforms, Ceausescu turned a corner and sacrificed the welfare of the Romanians to his personal greed and his contempt for them. His violent end spoke loudly to the world about the fate of those who abuse others and was, as it were, seen as writing on the wall.

Belshazzar was an abusive leader in his day. It was not a televised image that announced his end, however. It was a hand that mysteriously appeared and wrote the words *Mene, Mene, Tekel,* and *Parsin* on the wall of the hall where he banqueted (Daniel 5:25). Belshazzar was so frightened that his "face turned pale, and his thoughts terrified him. His limbs gave way, and his knees knocked together" (Daniel 5:6).

Of the wise men he consulted, only Daniel could translate the message for him. It meant that Belshazzar had been weighed in the balance and found wanting, that his days were numbered, and that his kingdom would be divided and given to others.

Whether the story is historical or not, it is instructive. Modern communist leaders had to realize that, when measured, they certainly would be found lacking and their days were possibly just as numbered as those of their fallen despots in arms, the Ceausescus.

Belshazzar was slain, a new government installed, and great reforms occurred in the wake of his downfall. The story is the same. Only the times and the names have changed.

CHAPTER 20

I Know That My Redeemer Lives!

I know that my redeemer lives!" These beautiful words of trust sustain us through the cold dark winter of despair until spring wraps us once again in the warm embrace of a promise fulfilled. Once we accept without doubt the mystery of the resurrection, like the wondrous return of new budding life following winter, we achieve a blessed union of spirit and body.

Some seek this perfect union of spirit and body through the pursuit of material wealth, fame, or the comfort of success in the belief that earthly reward will grant total happiness. But I have come to doubt that worldly means alone are sufficient. My conviction that true joy is not dependent upon worldly means was reinforced for me one Easter when I witnessed the jubilation of thousands of faithful believers who rushed through the shards of a ruined nation and failed ideology to experience the delight of unimpeded worship in the remains of their churches. That moving Easter event took place in 1991, when the bells of the Orthodox churches in Russia were first allowed to ring again and Easter processions with icons resumed, unrestrained by the harassment of past years.

Orthodox Easter Vigil that Saturday night in Moscow was launched with grand processions outside the churches, joined by thousands of Muscovites. Swept through the streets late that night by throngs of people while trying to get close enough to witness events first hand, I came upon an old woman perched quietly on a broken wooden crate, waiting on the side of a darkened street. Clad in a worn and shapeless coat, her head wrapped in a colorful but faded shawl, she sat smiling in the dim streetlight. It was nearly 11 P.M. on Easter Eve and the woman sat unaware of the surrounding dirt and garbage, her face shining as if in sunlight. Astonished by her apparent happiness, I stopped, compelled to speak with her, and asked if we were near the place where the Easter Vigil procession would begin to the Church of Saint Gabriel the Archangel.

The woman smiled warmly and invited me to sit by her on a second crate. In the late evening darkness she began to describe to me, an obvious foreigner, the significance of the return of the *Krestniy hod*, the holy procession about to commence around the church that, she indicated, was just ahead. She described the event with the expectation and excitement of a child at Christmas and explained how, since the 1917 revolution, Easter processions had been banned altogether and the church bell towers committed to silence.

In the dim light, the woman related how long ago as a child she had carried a candle in the procession each year, and later had sung in the massed choirs. With the country in a state of near civil war and economic collapse, there was little to eat and virtually nothing in the stores.

"We have little on our tables and less in our hands," she whispered. "But now," she confided, eyes shining with unrestrained joy, "we have the freedom to celebrate the Easter resurrection as we did in the past, and, my friend, that's all we need."

With a broad, gold-toothed smile, she jumped from the crate and enacted the procession, holding an imaginary icon in the air triumphantly above her head. She danced and twirled like a young ballerina, then suddenly stopped, glanced at the clock on the wall nearby, and motioned me away. "Hurry, you'll miss the blessings."

I wandered toward the gathering crowd, dazed by what I had seen, and watched the chanted blessing and the beginning of the procession of thousands of shuffling citizens. Most wore nondescript clothing, but I spotted the odd tuxedo and evening gown here and there among the working coveralls and the occasional uniforms of police and soldiers whose red-star-emblazoned caps were removed in reverence. Engulfed by the crowd, I was swept inside the church and surrounded by hundreds of candles whose gold light was reflected from gilded icons. Deep chanting in rich harmony rose from voices hidden somewhere in the arched ceiling blackened by years of candle smoke. I was nearly overcome by the strong incense and the close scent of humanity.

By chance I spotted a familiar worn coat and colorful kerchief in the mass of people wedged inside the crowded church and immediately recognized the wearer as the same happy woman I had spoken with. She was stooping to show a young child in the crowd how to make the sign of the cross in the proper Orthodox fashion. As she straightened, she by chance turned toward me and caught my eye. Her face burst into a brilliant smile of recognition with the same light I had seen on the street corner. Then in the glow of the candles, it seemed her face was gradually transformed into that of beautiful young woman, belying the gray strands poking from beneath the kerchief, her bent figure, and wrinkled hands.

She pushed her way toward me through the crushing crowd. When she reached me, she smiled triumphantly and whispered in my ear, "You see my friend, Christ is risen."

In my best Russian I answered, "He has risen indeed," and the bells began a cacophony of metallic chiming mixed with the pure tones of the choir. The chanting swelled and as the woman turned to the altar she quickly thrust an object into my hand.

Dazed by the overwhelming emotion of the scene, I stood frozen in that beautiful moment of total joy as the crowd rejoiced in their new right to celebrate Easter with overwhelming delight and freedom. When I finally recovered, the woman had faded into the crowd. I looked down at the object she had passed to me and saw it was a red egg, the Orthodox symbol of the resurrection.

In retrospect, the padded seats, soft kneelers, and heated comfort of our own churches today—and all the superficial conflicts that plague their day-to-day administration—suddenly shrink before the greater gift of the freedom to celebrate the resurrection as we choose.

Biblical Reflection

At that moment [Anna] came, and began to praise God and to speak about the child to all who were looking for the redemption of Jerusalem. Luke 2:38

Once an old woman waited her whole life in great anticipation of the savior. Her name was Anna, which means "grace." This Anna, who was known as a prophetess, was in the temple in Jerusalem on the day Mary and Joseph brought the baby Jesus to be presented to the Lord according to custom.

An old man named Simeon had taken Jesus in his arms and declared:

> Master, now you are dismissing your servant in peace,
> according to your word;
> for my eyes have seen your salvation,
> which you have prepared in the presence of all peoples,
> a light for revelation to the Gentiles
> and for glory to your people Israel. Luke 2:29-32

Anna, hearing the words and seeing the child, gave thanks to God and she talked about him to people who were looking for hope and salvation.

Some two thousand years later, another old woman, living in the apparent spiritual desolation of Moscow, waited most of her life for the return of freedom to worship her Lord openly. It turns out that all along, despite the political climate that severely limited and overtly discouraged her worship, she had treasured within herself the sure knowledge of her redeemer. Like Anna, even as an old woman, she was only too glad to share what she knew with others who were seeking redemption.

This old Muscovite held cherished memories of childhood candlelight vigils. She knew what to do and what to expect when once again she was afforded the opportunity to join in public worship. She, with many thousands of others, showed the light that had been burning all along in their nation, though the shadows of oppression had closed in about them for years.

There are too many instances in history where public worship has been denied and people have grown old waiting. The waiting of the old, however, is a powerful thing. Not all the thousands in the crowded streets on that night in 1991 were old. All ages were present and all joined in crying out, "Christ is risen! He is risen indeed!"

How did the young know? They knew because of two key things. First, they knew because it is true—he is risen. He is risen indeed, and he is alive and present in our world. And second, they knew because the old ones, while waiting with hope in the shadows, dared to share their faith in whatever ways they could in defiance of the oppressor.

It is not easy to be old and poor and lacking the basic necessities of life. Nevertheless, that voice at Easter urging others on with, "Hurry, you'll miss the blessing," was as strong as Anna's—despite the attempts to silence her witness.

CHAPTER 21

Red Banners Furled

arly Christmas morning, 1991, the phone woke me in my Moscow River apartment. Captain Lev Vtorygin, former Soviet naval officer, military intelligence officer, and long-time friend, was on the line. In a voice charged with excitement he insisted we meet to observe a monumental event. Mikhail Gorbachev had resigned the day before and I was expecting the unusual.

Lev wanted to meet at first light on Red Square near the Spassky gate. I donned my fur hat and overcoat and walked the three kilometers to Red Square through the frozen morning. Snow flurries blew across the Moscow River and stung my face as I trudged along the deserted embankment, leaning into the cold wind and wondering what was up. My breath froze in short clouds of mist as I walked in the early light. The sky turned a brilliant pink as the sun rose through the broken puffy clouds. Moscow was at its best in the early morning hours when the streets were empty.

I arrived at a nearly deserted Red Square. Only the gray overcoats and fur shapkas of the Kremlin guards were visible, moving slowly on the square. I could make out the broad figure of Lev standing with his back against the black wrought-iron fence on the west side of St Basil's. He was looking high above the top of the Lenin mausoleum. Lev saw me, waved, and began to walk toward me.

"Look up there." I noticed frosted tears smeared across his ruddy face as he walked toward me. "It's gone. Look!"

I turned to follow his gesture. High atop the Kremlin dome fluttered an oversized white, blue, and red Russian tri-color! The solid red flag of the U.S.S.R. with its hammer and sickle was gone! I could neither speak nor further see the flag as my eyes filled. The two of us stood in Red Square in the early sunrise and blowing snow, two former naval intelligence officers, one Russian, the other American.

The Kremlin guards watched in silence and stomped their feet in the light snow. The Soviet Union was no more. On all Soviet warships that day, throughout an empire that extended over ten time zones and two continents, the ancient Russian naval blue and white cross of St. Andrew replaced the Soviet naval ensign. The red jack with hammer and sickle was stowed, and all red banners furled. Lenin's experiment had ended; the Soviet Navy was no more.

Three years earlier, I had begun an assignment in Moscow as the senior U.S. naval attaché, a tour of duty that capped years of study of the Soviet Navy and launched a personal involvement in Russia that spanned the second Russian Revolution and the ebb of Soviet communism. The U.S. naval attaché post in the U.S.S.R. had a long history of high adventure and intrigue beginning with navy Commander Hugo Koehler, who traveled in disguise throughout Russia, reporting on Bolshevik activities during the Civil War of the 1920s.

Koehler, who was sent to southern Russia as a special agent by the U.S. State Department to observe and report on the Soviet threat firsthand, possessed extraordinary courage and unusual strategic vision. His assignment was to "find out . . . whether Bolshevism is a real force, a workable idea, one that will endure, or whether it is the false doctrine it appears to be."[1] On that frosty morning in Red Square seventy-one years and many attachés later, I sensed Koehler's assigned question was finally answered.

Biblical Reflection

Then the LORD said, "I have observed the misery of my people who are in Egypt; I have heard their cry on account of their taskmasters. Indeed, I know their sufferings, and I have come down to deliver them from the Egyptians, and to bring them up out of that land to a good and broad land, a land flowing with milk and honey. Exodus 3:7-8

The story of the Assyrian King Sennacherib occurs in biblical texts, in the writings of Herodotus, and in the writings of the king himself. He was a force to be reckoned with, and he gained control of extensive lands, demanding payment of tribute from all the peoples he conquered. He was following in the footsteps of previous Assyrian kings who had already scattered ten of the tribes of Israel.

Hezekiah, king of Judah, tried to resist Sennacherib and ended up losing most of his own cities. Even though he attempted to hold on to Jerusalem at all costs, he finally capitulated and agreed to pay tribute. Sennacherib decided to invade the city anyway.

Sennacherib boastfully taunted Hezekiah's people by asking, "Has any of the gods of the nations saved their land out of the hand of the king of Assyria?" (Isaiah 36:18).

Hezekiah was determined to resist, lest one more tribe of Israel be lost. He convinced his people to stand firm despite the formidable odds. Though Sennacherib proclaimed himself invincible, Hezekiah was determined that his culture and his people survive, and he turned to his faith to inspire and sustain Jerusalem while he worked on its behalf.

In fact, Sennacherib did not succeed against Jerusalem. Both the Bible and Herodotus speak of a disaster that destroyed thousands of Assyrian troops. Sennacherib himself returned home to Ninevah where he was later slain by two of his own sons.

We are not meant to be enslaved. No matter what guise covers the enslavement, governments that attempt to distort the human spirit in a quest for the glory of one or a few oppressive leaders are doomed to fail. The timelines may vary, and the circumstances be unique, but with certainty, some leader or vision will arise and remind men and women of their own humanity—and every idol will topple and every flag of oppression be furled.

CHAPTER 22

My Brother's Keeper

My German friend Uwe Mahrenholtz is a happy and outgoing man. Despite spending his youth in a war-torn country, he seems always to look at the brighter side of life. He was born in Dresden, before the terrible bombing, and grew up in wartime Berlin. A British Spitfire shot down his father, an air force pilot, over the English Channel while he was returning from a bombing mission over England. His body washed up on a beach in Denmark and is buried there in a German military cemetery.

I first met Uwe in Moscow in 1988, where, as a German Navy captain, he served as naval attaché in the West German Embassy. In the coming years we would experience together the dramatic fall of the Berlin Wall and the collapse of communism in the Soviet Union.

Uwe had visited the United States as a young man and had been captivated by the American culture of freedom and the easygoing way of life. He became a fan of popular country-and-western music, wore his blond hair in a 1950s crew cut, and envied life in the American West.

As a young officer in the new West German Navy in 1959, Uwe accompanied a crew to the U.S. naval base in Charleston, South Carolina, to accept the transfer of a squadron of six Fletcher-class destroyers the United States had given to the fledgling West German Navy. Uwe was slated to be a junior officer aboard the former USS *Wadsworth*, a seasoned but still solid ship.

At that time, the navy base in Charleston was separated from the city by a troubled section of town that had become the focus of civil rights protests and ugly riots. The base was surrounded by a ghetto inhabited mostly by poor and angry African Americans. The German crews, as well as all American military personnel, had been warned and ordered not to wander alone into the town, and to leave the base only on supervised tours.

After months of training, and with the date for his squadron's departure approaching, Uwe realized he had yet to take photos of the city. Thus, on the last Sunday morning before sailing, he ventured forth from the base, alone and in civilian clothes, to take pictures of the city. Despite the warnings, Uwe unwisely proceeded through the streets of the surrounding area to find his way into downtown Charleston. As he strolled, eventually losing his way, he noticed a group of several young black men following him. At first he paid little attention, but he soon noticed that they seemed angry. They began to pelt him with stones and he began to sense that he was in serious trouble.

Alarmed, Uwe tried to find his way back to the base, but only became more confused and more lost. The crowd behind him gradually grew, becoming loud and boisterous. Uwe began to run; frightened he might never find the base. His pursuers brandished sticks and gained on him quickly as he ran in panic through the deserted streets surrounded by dilapidated houses and burned-out buildings.

Desperately seeking refuge, Uwe spotted a church ahead. He heard the deep sounds of powerful singing. It was about 11 A.M. when the frightened young German dashed up the steps of a Baptist church and yanked open the doors. The crowd of angry men behind him stopped short of the steps and watched as Uwe burst into the building out of breath.

Uwe froze in the doorway; the church was packed with black people. A sermon was in progress and the entire congregation turned to watch the unusual spectacle of a lone white man, with blond crew cut, standing in the door, wearing a loudly colored tourist shirt, camera hanging on his shoulder. The noise of the angry mob behind him stilled suddenly.

The preacher, a large, burly black man with elegant white hair, stopped in mid-sermon. Observing the situation and sensing the tension, the preacher invited the frightened young man to approach the chancel. Uwe followed the pastor's beckoning and walked up to the pulpit while hundreds of curious eyes followed his steps.

After Uwe arrived at the pulpit and mounted the stairs, the preacher put his arm around his shoulders and began an extemporaneous talk on brotherly love. He spoke of how people should put away the prejudices of the modern world and abide by the ancient teachings of the Bible. When he finished, a chorus of amens rang out. Uwe was then invited to explain his situation to the congregation.

The pastor then invited Uwe to a coffee gathering in the church's fellowship hall. After a time of cordial conversation the pastor summoned two large men and said, "Take this man and escort him to safety, as Christ would in this case. Do not hesitate to use your stout force to ensure this child of God is delivered to safety, as Christ's disciples certainly would have done. Go in peace and praise the Lord."

By this time thoroughly confused and scared, Uwe followed the two men, who could easily have been linemen from a professional football team, as they escorted him through the crowd and out of the church. The throng of pursuers, still clutching their clubs and knives, parted as the three men ventured forth toward the safety of the base.

In 1976, Uwe recorded his experience for an essay contest sponsored by a German magazine for the two-hundreth anniversary of American independence. For his essay, he was awarded two tickets to New York. Uwe took his wife to New York and then to Charleston to locate the church from which he had been rescued. Unfortunately, Charleston had recently been devastated by a hurricane and the church was no longer there.

Biblical Reflection

Blessed rather are those who hear the word of God and obey it!
Luke 11:28

Two groups of people, those outside the church and those inside the church, acted because of the presence of a stranger among them. The meeting of two groups of blacks and a lone white man in the American South of 1959 could have had any number of outcomes, but due to the presence of one more man, the peaceful outcome triumphed.

Those inside the church were able to turn around a life-threatening event and perhaps even provide a sermon-in-action to those outside the church because of the other man present. That other man was Jesus.

During his life on earth, Jesus was present more than once when mob anger burned through a crowd. He once saved a woman caught in adultery and about to be stoned by the men who accused her. He had escaped himself when angry people gathered to throw him from a cliff in his own hometown. He was cruelly scourged and then hung from the cross as a chorus of angry voices shouted, "Crucify him! Crucify him!" Jesus knew about crowds and hatred and anger. And in 1959, Jesus acted to save Uwe Mahrenholtz. Am I serious? Absolutely. It was Jesus in that Baptist church.

A church building is, in some ways, like one of the six cities of refuge described in the Old Testament. According to Numbers 35, a person, even a complete stranger, who was accused of slaying someone could escape to a city of refuge and be safe until his case was heard. If it turned out he had unintentionally caused the death of someone, he could remain safe in the city of refuge for as long as he lived. He could depend on fair treatment upon arrival, and then he could depend on being judged fairly during his stay (Numbers 35:9-15).

Such cities do not exist anymore, but many people recognize a church building as a place of potential refuge and help. Mahrenholtz wisely sought refuge in the familiarity of a church, though he soon discovered that the faces inside were as different from his as those outside. Those inside, however, had an advantage over the angry faces outside. These were the faces of witnesses.

To make the choice to be at worship on a Sunday morning is to be a witness. It is witnessing to one's will to be part of a community, to be part of a fellowship bound by the laws of God. It is witnessing to the fact that one is willing to learn— and to pay—the costs of discipleship. It is witnessing to one's will to change oneself in order to be aligned with God's plans and purposes. Such were the people whose eyes followed Mahrenholtz as he walked toward the pulpit.

It was not the first time the congregation raised its voice to say "Amen" to the pastor's remarks. The pastor would have been surprised to *not* hear his teaching encouraged by those voices. When he finally called some stout men forward to act as escorts for Mahrenholtz, he knew they would obey his leadership and do the right thing. He did not have to be afraid. He had already brought the Word of life to the people in front of him. This was not the first day they had met, we can be sure. When he spoke with passion from his pulpit, he spoke words with the authority of Jesus and brought his people to recognize in Mahrenholtz a child of God among them. He made the image of Christ clear to those who heard his words. All he had to do was remind those present of this Word of God, and impress upon them the need to keep it, to walk in the Word without compromise. That whole congregation could have been called on to escort Mahrenholtz through the unfamiliar and unfriendly streets, and no doubt would have. But only two were needed it seems.

Could two men face down an angry crowd? These churchmen could, because with the light and authority of Jesus, and with the power of his command to love the neighbor, they could look their angry brothers and neighbors in the eye and say, "He is with us. We are in Christ. We hear and obey his Word and act as this man's refuge." Those inside the church made a tremendous difference in Mahrenholtz's life and future.

Cain almost flippantly asked God, "Am I my brother's keeper?" The answer is always yes—and we look to the church to keep the answer in front of us.

CHAPTER 23

The *Matryushka* Doll

The following encounter was but one of a series of moving events that took place during four days of spectacular firsts. In July 1989, the United States and Soviet navies traded warship visits for the first time in seventeen years. The recommencement was a part of the confidence-building measures dreamed up by then-chairman of the U.S. Joint Chiefs of Staff, Admiral William Crowe, and the late Marshal Sergei Akhromeev, chief of the Soviet General Staff. The measures were devised to help ease slowly away from decades of mistrust, when both sides regarded each other as their next wartime enemy. The events were often dramatic and sometimes replete with surprise.

Preparing for the visit was a monumental task for U.S Embassy personnel in Moscow. The visit would unleash hundreds of young American sailors into Sevastopol, a city that, for the most part, had not been visited by foreigners since the Bolsheviks drove out the failed remnants of the White Russian Army in 1921, at the end of the Russian Civil War. Sevastopol is a gleaming city of sun-bleached white buildings. It was the main port and headquarters for the Red Banner Soviet Black Sea Fleet.

The first stumbling block for the embassy was giving the U.S. government a fair assessment of the security situation anticipated during the visit. Sevastopol was considered a closed military city, and even Soviet citizens could visit only by special permission. The city, in true Soviet fashion of that day, sported no "strip," as most free-world ports did. There were no red light districts, no bars, and few hotels considered by Soviet authorities as suitable for foreigners.

When the embassy naval attaché predicted in writing that the Americans would probably be treated well and in traditional Russian fashion, the security organs of Washington, D.C, immediately challenged him. They argued that the Soviets would take every opportunity to compromise the young American sailors; they would be drugged and probably assaulted by the notorious KGB. It had to be so; it had been so for seventy years.

Not so, argued the embassy. These events were far too important for the developing relations between the two countries. Nevertheless, the embassy agreed to a two-man buddy system, so at least two sailors would face together the anticipated abuse.

The day came with a grand display of hospitality unmatched in many years of navy port visits. Two ships from the U.S. Sixth Fleet came into the Black Sea from the Mediterranean and moored against the downtown seawall at the famed Potemkin Steps, named after the infamous Russian battleship on which a mutiny occurred during the revolution. The city glistened and crowds of hundreds turned out to watch the arrival. For four days the city seemed a constant carnival—shops were closed, no work was done—as the Russians went about showing off their renowned hospitality. (More than eighty percent of the inhabitants of Sevastopol are Russian despite the fact that the Crimea is part of the Ukraine, the result of a long and typically complex bit of Soviet history.)

The Soviet host fleet did well keeping the American sailors busy on tours, visiting famous battle sites, and attending gala concerts and traditional feasts. The hosts were careful to allow the sailors some time for independent shore liberty as requested by the ships' commanders. It was astounding what happened, or what didn't happen. There was not one case of misbehavior on the part of the visiting sailors and not a single incident of hostility between the hosts and visitors, despite the fact they had been training to fight one another for more than fifty years. The U.S. ambassador was there with his wife and a gaggle of embassy staff, grateful to be in such a pleasant setting and away from the drab grayness of Moscow.

One unforgettable event transpired the second day of the visit. Long lines of curious citizens formed early in the morning for tours of the American ships. The navy was well prepared for the crowds and provided guided tours, culminating with typical American picnic fare of hot dogs and hamburgers with homemade ice cream for all. By eight in the morning the lines of visiting Russians stretched well out of sight. The naval attaché left the cruiser for a meeting at a local hotel to look after details of the protocol event to be held that same evening, a reception for the seniors, officers, and petty officers of the visiting ships and their Soviet hosts. Dressed in summer tropical whites, he crossed the large square while Russian men, women, and children stared in typical disciplined silence.

Suddenly, a young girl broke from near the end of one line and walked bravely up to the attaché. She was dressed in a starched white dress and wore a red bow in her plaited hair—a frequent custom when observing a holiday.

"Are you an American, sir?" she asked boldly.

"Yes, I am," the officer replied.

"Well, see, I'm way back there in the line and I don't think I'll ever be able to get on the ship. I want to give an American a gift, so I'll just give it to you." And she reached out her hand and proffered a tiny wooden *matryushka* doll about the size of a walnut.

"Here," she said, "it's from me, I'm Russian." Before the astounded officer could reply, the girl had vanished back into the crowd.

After the visit, in an interview shown on Soviet television, a young American was asked how he and his shipmates had been treated during the four-day visit to Sevastopol.

"Well," said the sailor, "these people treated us better than our allies do when we visit."

Biblical Reflection

The wolf shall live with the lamb, the leopard shall lie down with the kid, the calf and the lion and the fatling together, and a little child shall lead them. Isaiah 11:6

Whoever becomes humble like this child is the greatest in the kingdom of heaven. Whoever welcomes one such child in my name welcomes me. If any of you put a stumbling block before one of these little ones who believe in me, it would be better for you if a great millstone were fastened around your neck and you were drowned in the depth of the sea. Matthew 18:4-6

In Isaiah 9:6 we read, "For a child has been born for us, a son given to us; authority rests upon his shoulders; and he is named Wonderful Counselor, Mighty God, Everlasting Father, Prince of Peace." While these words foreshadow the coming of the Messiah, they also give a succinct picture of the role of good government. The image presented is one of a person shouldering responsibility in a way that reflects sound counsel and that leads to just authority, good judgment, order, and peace.

It is striking that in her quest to present a small gift to an American, a little Russian girl unknowingly selected an official who had some measure of influence over future policies affecting her country's relations with the United States. The entire vignette of a child breaking out of a disciplined line and approaching an American suggests the hope and innocence of children around the world, those whom all governments have a duty to protect, following the admonition in Romans 12:18: "If it is possible, so far as it depends on you, live peaceably with all."

Ambassadors, attachés, planners, and others in authority, while looking to maintain advantageous balances in economic and strategic positions, can do no better than to keep in mind that they bear on their shoulders the onus of decisions that will affect the quality of individual lives in profound ways. Whether iron curtains descend or states are balkanized or nations and regions are gripped by despotic political systems that victimize countless persons depends in large part on the long-range vision of those in authority who help to shape policy, who write and enforce treaties, who negotiate the agreements that ultimately determine many of the freedoms and opportunities others enjoy or are denied. Those at the tables of accord, seeking to prevail in their own views of order in the world, can benefit from the wisdom of Winston Churchill, who declared:

> The right to guide the course of world history is the noblest prize of victory. We are still toiling up the hill; we have not yet reached the crest-line of it; we cannot survey the landscape or even imagine what its condition will be when that longed-for morning comes. The task that lies before us immediately is at once more practical, simpler and sterner. I hope—indeed I pray—that we shall not be found unworthy of our victory if after toil and tribulation it is granted to us. For the rest, we have to gain the victory. That is our task."[1]

Like so many other Churchill speeches that incorporated biblical wisdom, the words above are imbued with the wisdom and imagery of Malachi 4:2: "But for you who revere my name the sun of righteousness shall rise, with healing in its wings. You shall go out leaping like calves from the stall." Churchill spoke of the longed-for morning that would end World War II with an Allied victory, and Churchill is the person who popularized the term *iron curtain* as the Cold War made itself felt throughout the world.

In 1989, a little girl, red ribbons tied neatly in her hair, skipping like a calf, white dress shining in the sunlight, was a vivid symbol of the power of penetrating light. Indeed, she symbolized another of the great statesman's visions that one day nations "will plan and build in justice, in tradition, and in freedom a house of many mansions where there will be room for all," an image he borrowed from Jesus Christ himself.[2]

CHAPTER 24

A Church Returned

T o those faithful Westerners in Moscow, July 14, 1991, was a remarkable day. Just a month before the attempted coup against Soviet General Secretary Mikhail Gorbachev, which precipitated the dissolution of the Soviet Union, the English-owned Anglican church of Saint Andrew's opened it doors again for the Holy Eucharist with the sound of sacred music filling the rafters after seventy-two years of silence.

The history of St. Andrew's is long and complex. The congregation can be traced back to the sixteenth century during the reign of Ivan IV (Ivan the Terrible) of Russia. It was he who initially gave permission for foreign communities trading with Russia to build their own church buildings.

Over the next three centuries, the English Russia Company paved the way for business ventures in the frozen reaches of darkest Russia. To serve these business pioneers, a first Anglican chaplaincy was established in Archangel in the seventeenth century. Moscow remained a very small community and most foreigners lived in St. Petersburg, the capital, where an Anglican church was opened in 1754. Its chaplain served both the capital and Moscow.

In 1825, Tsar Alexander I authorized the construction of a church in Moscow "with the same privileges" as those in other cities in Russia. So the British built a small chapel in central Moscow on the ground where St. Andrew's stands today, less than five hundred yards from the Kremlin. In 1882, with the

foreign presence in Moscow growing in step with the burgeoning of trade with Russia, the Bishop of London authorized the construction of a church, officially designating it
The British Church of St. Andrew, Moscow. It was completed
and consecrated in 1885.

The structure itself is not remarkable. Built by British
business interests, its Victorian Gothic, red brick tower juts
proudly upward between the onion-domed Russian Orthodox
churches dominating the Moscow skyline. When constructed,
the tower was forbidden to receive chimes—only Russian
Orthodox churches were permitted bells. So the congregation
used the belfry tower to store valuables and records. Through
its long history, the building has been used as a nanny dormi-
tory, stable, a Bolshevik machine-gun nest, and, alternately,
a place of worship for foreigners, until it was made the official studio for the Soviet State classical recording enterprise
Melodiya. The church's remarkable acoustics made it a perfect
fit for Melodiya and gave the Soviet government an excuse to
keep pesky foreign worshipers at bay.

Beginning with the October Revolution in 1917, more
than 400,000 churches were destroyed in all of Russia. Bolshevik vandals, following the dictum of the Soviet system,
destroyed most of these parishes. But curiously, many of the
vandals first hacked out and stole millions of icons, stashing
them away in the hope of better years. Those churches not
robbed and pillaged by over-enthusiastic communists were
destroyed during World War II.

The number 400,000 seems at first exaggerated, but given
the history of complete domination of the Russian people by
the dysfunctional Tsars and the intolerant Russian Orthodox
Church, the number becomes realistic. There were churches,
chapels, shrines, and icons everywhere, from the far reaches
of Siberia to the Crimea on the Black Sea.

The last Anglican chaplain at St. Andrew's before it
descended into its cold seventy years of disuse was Frank
North. One of his sons recalled the fateful events of 1917,

when "the Bolsheviks set up a machine-gun post in one of the attics, and our family was forced to spend a week in the basement with no light and little food. Emerging from our dungeon when the fighting stopped, we discovered piles of spent cartridges in the courtyard and two large pools of blood."[1]

North remained in Moscow until March 1920, when, after assisting the evacuation of the British community, and after several imprisonments, he was allowed to flee to Helsinki, where he accepted the chaplaincy called "Helsinki with Moscow." The St. Andrew's chaplaincy continued to reside in Finland. When relations warmed periodically, the chaplain was allowed to enter the Soviet Union to conduct services, usually in either the British ambassador's office or the ornate U.S. ambassador's residence off Moscow's Garden Ring Road.

In the late 1980s, a new attempt to regain the use of St. Andrew's for regular worship was begun by a handful of members of the British and American communities. Regular worship in a real church was increasingly sought after for both the Moscow-based diplomats and the few hardscrabble Western business folks brave enough to work in the U.S.S.R.

The process to regain use of the church, despite its checkered background, was fraught with high drama. A few determined parishioners led by two naval attachés, one British, the other American, resurrected a previously failed effort that had run into the stonewall of Soviet bureaucracy and obfuscation. With the new openness of Soviet General Secretary Mikhail Gorbachev, these folks began knocking on countless new doors, only to be informed that they must appeal to the Soviet Committee on Religious Affairs, staffed and run by the KGB. They did exactly that and were astounded to hear that the request to regain use of the church must first be forwarded to the Central Committee of the Communist Party, an obvious tactic to thwart the effort.

It was May 1988, and the Reagan-Gorbachev summit was approaching, as was the millennium celebration—the one-thousandth anniversary of Christianity in Russia. There was new hope for all believers. If the St. Andrew's vestry could just get a request through ahead of time to President Reagan, he might be persuaded to bring up the matter in a private session with Gorbachev. However, to do so would require more clout than the small vestry of St. Andrew's could muster.

Help came from unlikely allies—first in the form of the staunchly Roman Catholic Philippine ambassador in Moscow, who suggested he call a meeting of all foreign ambassadors willing to help. (A large number of St. Andrew's parishioners were Anglicans and Episcopalians from other countries, including many from Africa.) Deftly awaiting the absence of the *doyen*, who was North Korean, the ambassadors met, presided over by the acting *doyen*, the ambassador of Nigeria, himself a Muslim.

Twenty-one ambassadors signed a petition addressed to President Reagan asking him to raise the issue of the church building in his coming meetings with the Soviet leader. U.S. Ambassador Jack Matlock carried the petition when he flew out to Helsinki to fly in with President Reagan.

To this day, no one really knows what passed between the two leaders. But three years later, the wily and many-termed mayor of Moscow, Yuri Lushkov, apparently moved by divine intervention, or most likely a shove from the new Kremlin leadership, summoned the St. Andrew's vestry committee and announced that St. Andrew's could be used for worship in perpetuity while the ownership of the building could be discussed later.

That sunny Sunday morning in July 1991, St. Andrew's Anglican Chaplain Tyler Strand opened the first service in seventy-two years with a blessing in the courtyard. Then a crucifer and two altar boys led a procession of grateful worshipers into St. Andrew's Moscow to the strains of "All Creatures of Our God and King." Three years later, after considerable growth and continuing struggle with Russian bureaucracy, Queen Elizabeth II joined a service in St. Andrew's during her visit to Russia.

Biblical Reflection

Who of you is left who saw this house in its former glory? How does it look to you now? Does it not seem to you like nothing? But now be strong . . . "Be strong all you people of the land," declares the LORD, "and work. For I am with you," declares the LORD Almighty. "This is what I covenanted with you when you came out of Egypt. And my Spirit remains among you. Do not fear."

This is what the LORD Almighty says: "In a little while I will once more shake the heavens and the earth, and the sea and dry land. I will shake all nations, and the desired of all nations will come, and I will fill this house with glory," says the LORD Almighty. "The silver is mine and the gold is mine," declares the LORD Almighty. "The glory of this present house will be greater than the glory of the for-mer house," says the LORD Almighty. "And in this place I will grant peace," declares the LORD Almighty. Haggai 2:3-9 NIV

And God took people from among the nations, from the land and from the sea, and restored St. Andrew's, and brought peace, and his Spirit remained.

CHAPTER 25

A Long Walk

Ebensee is a town of roughly six thousand inhabitants nestled in the Alps sixty kilometers southeast of Saltzburg. The picturesque town sits astride a mountain lake in the cradle of the Saltzkammergut, site of the jolly *Sound of Music*. But aside from the flowers, cows, *lederhosen*-clad yodelers, and romantic kitsch of the musical, there lies hidden in the area a more sinister place reminding visitors of the dark and murderous deeds of the Nazi machine a mere sixty-five years ago. Across the rail tracks from Ebensee center lie the remains of a concentration camp, one of more than forty satellite camps spread like sinister webs throughout the country from the main horror camp at Mauthausen in northeast Austria.

In 1943, shortly after the Allied bombing of the German rocket research center, test range, and launch site at Peenemunde on the Baltic coast of Germany, Hitler and his henchmen decided to go underground with their burgeoning missile construction program. Ebensee was selected as the second site for digging a massive array of tunnels where the missiles would be assembled and tested. The first site was located in the Hartz mountains near Nordhausen in central Germany.

These missiles included the dreaded A4, known as the V2, killing tool for thousands of British and Belgian war dead, and the advanced A6 and A9, known as the Amerikarockets, which, when completed, could target the United States. Using the natural cover of the rugged mountains, the plan fit hand-in-glove with the construction of other tunnel complexes in Hitler's Alpine redoubt. The demented leader considered these underground tunnels more secure from the Allied control of the air.

It was at the memorial site commemorating more than eight thousand victims who perished at the Ebensee camp in the last two years of the war that I observed two figures—a man and a woman—kneeling before a mass grave marker. The man, Stephan Wolfe, was saying *kaddish* for his father. The woman recited a psalm. What follows is the story of Stephan Wolfe's father.

In late 1942, David Wolfe left his rural home in northern Germany for a short walk. He never returned. He, a Jew, and his devoted Christian wife had taken the prudent but painful step of legally divorcing, despite their deep mutual love, in order to best protect their two children—a son of two and a daughter of six. Wolfe found temporary haven in the home of friends who hid his identity while he worked in an agricultural job. He then disappeared without a trace for sixty-four years.

The remainder of the Wolfe family survived the war and thereafter began the nearly impossible search for their father. Only in June 2006 did the son, Stephan, learn from a Holocaust database in Israel that his father had been placed in the Auschwitz death camp. Combing the meticulous SS records at Auschwitz, Stephan learned the German Army had taken his father from the camp just one week prior to its liberation in 1945. He and a large group of the healthiest prisoners were force-marched eighty miles southwest and finally herded aboard rail stockcars and transported to Mauthausen in Austria. Prison camp documents at Mauthausen, meticulous records of the Nazi's filthy deeds, showed Wolfe was further transported to the satellite camp at Ebensee to work on the tunnels for the new underground missile program. Son Stephan learned that day in October 2006 that his father's name was listed on an Ebensee report sent to the lead camp at Mauthausen, stating that in March 1945 David Wolfe had died of "heart failure."

Indeed, most of those in the reports of more than eight thousand dead were listed as either "killed while trying to escape" or "died of heart failure." "Heart failure" was most likely due to a mix of starvation, exhaustion, and disease.

Stephan seemed to have surmised how his father's story would end and here it was, corroborated in an old, yellowing report. He told me of his sixty-year search. Now he would go home to Berlin and write to the entire family, spread from Israel to Germany to the United States. With tear-reddened eyes he told me, "It was a long walk for my father, and a long walk for me."

Biblical Reflection

On the day that you stood aside, on the day that strangers carried off his wealth, and foreigners entered his gates and cast lots for Jerusalem, you too were like one of them. Obadiah 1:11

Viktor Frankl, gifted psychiatrist and death camp survivor, was imprisoned in Auschwitz, perhaps during the same time that it appears David Wolfe was a prisoner. His seminal book, *Man's Search for Meaning*, is a stark account of privations, depravity, and death inside the camp environment, but it is also a testament to hope for humanity. In his book, he described the lives and sometimes the deaths of those whom he recognized as decent men, including a few of the guards.

In Frankl's mind, all human beings could be divided into just two basic types, those who were decent and those who were not. Frankl's insights, both as a man of faith and as a trained scientist of the mind, open windows of understanding on the behaviors and responses of the guards and the prisoners who lived in that hellish environment of the death camps.

One thing is clear: no decent human being could ever conceive of such an atrocity as a death camp, of ovens to consume human beings, of chambers to kill human beings with gas, of plans to starve human beings to death, of tormenting humans with unspeakable acts, of spitting in the face of God through such inhumane behavior. Indecent humans did this and, unfortunately, indecent human beings still attempt to visit such horrors on others around the world today.

The Bible records accounts of horrific behavior that rival that of the Nazis in their inhumanity. The valley of Hinnom, also known as Gehenna, is the site of the horror (2 Kings 16:3; 23:10; 2 Chronicles 28:3; and Jeremiah 7:31). In the valley of Hinnom, people—most often children—were burned to death in structures built specifically for this purpose.

As the Nazis had their ovens, these people created images of idols inside which they would build fires for consuming humans. The valley would be filled with the screams of dying children and with drumbeats intended to drown out the sound of their cries. Through prophets God condemned such human sacrifice as a detestable abomination. Over against the violence, the word from God was and is that we stop people who would perform such atrocities—that we stop hell on earth.

In ancient days, God's obedient servants were moved to destroy the means of human sacrifice and to rid the land of the idea that such practices could ever be acceptable. Gehenna is not an imaginary place. The vision of hell as a place of eternal fire and suffering is based on the real practices that took place in the historic valley of the sons of Hinnom. It is a place whose evil foreshadowed the Nazi atrocities. God's response to such evil is a loud and decisive "No!"—a response that must call God's people to act decisively against such evil.

God is the God of life, not of death. God is the God who demands decency, not indecency. Long after the practice of sacrificing children in fire had been wiped out, the valley of Hinnom, or Gehenna, remained such a defiled place that it was only used for burning refuse and unclean things—a garbage dump.

Frankl survived the death camps, though much of his life was taken away in the wasteland of Hitler's awful experiment. Frankl's witness, like that of many other prisoners, speaks to our deepest spiritual being and powerfully speaks of reasons to live and to hope. Even when confined to the bleak horrors of a concentration camp, even when suffering on account of others, even when trying to survive in the deepest shadows imaginable, there is a space in human beings that can be filled with the divine presence. Frankl discovered convictions, beliefs, and strengths that can keep a decent person decent despite every violent attempt to rob him or her of God-given dignity.

God is present within those who suffer, compelling the sufferer to live, to make it through his or her ordeal with the image of God intact. And God is present in the call to liberators to act on behalf of human decency.

In the Old Testament texts there are many accounts of God turning people away from evil practices that hurt others. Many times turning away evil involved using force to bring about change. While we do not offer a theology of war in this volume, we cannot escape the fact that God has called on warriors to liberate people and to bring justice out of injustice.

In the New Testament, Jesus is consistent in telling his followers to love the neighbor, love the enemy, do unto others as they would have done to them, forgive debts, live for the God of life and love, do not repay evil with evil. In James 2:15-17, we read: "If a brother or sister is naked and lacks daily food, and one of you says to them, 'Go in peace; keep warm and eat your fill,' and yet you do not supply their bodily needs, what is the good of that? So faith by itself, if it has no works, is dead." The works of faith include the works of justice.

Dietrich Bonhoeffer, a man of peace, observed:

It is an evil time when the world lets injustice happen silently, when the oppression of the poor and the wretched cries out to heaven in a loud voice and the judges and the rulers of the earth keep silent about it, when the persecuted church calls to God for help in the hour of dire distress and exhorts people to do justice, and yet no mouth on earth is opened to bring justice."[1]

To be truly human is to bear one another's burdens and honor life. That is the work of justice. Indeed, it is what it means to do justice, to love kindness, and to walk humbly with God (Micah 6:8).

Frankl wrote many words of wisdom that cannot be shared in these few lines, but it should be noted that he wrote poignantly of his love for his wife and how that love sustained him in the darkness of the camps. He wrote of how having the image in one's head of being loved by God or by a person who cares deeply for you can sustain one in the darkest hours and lead one away from disillusionment and toward hope, the essential key to survival.

The details of David Wolfe's last moments may be lost forever, but Wolfe's son and family lived. His son said *kaddish* for him. In divorcing the wife he loved, Wolfe hoped that she and their children might have a chance to live through the darkness and survive when the light triumphed. Such men have lived and live on through the hope they continue to inspire in other decent human beings.

Frankl makes the powerful observation at the end of *Man's Search for Meaning* that we have come to know "man as that being who has invented the gas chambers of Auschwitz; however, he is also the being who has entered those gas chambers upright with the Lord's Prayer or the *Shema Yisrael* on his lips."[2]

For decent people everywhere, responsible social action and, as Bonhoeffer proclaimed, "courageous intervention, and the readiness to suffer for what is acknowledged as right,"[3] help make the loving care of God credible. Who will stand, if not you and me?

ENDNOTES

Introduction

1. Dietrich Bonhoeffer, *Letters and Papers from Prison* (New York: Macmillan, 1972), 5.
2. Dietrich Bonhoeffer, *A Testament to Freedom: The Essential Writings of Dietrich Bonhoeffer,* ed Geffrey B. Kelly and F. Burton Nelson (San Francisco: HarperSanFrancisco, 1995), 285.

Chapter 8

1. Corrie ten Boom, *Tramp for the Lord* (Fort Washington, Pa.: Christian Literature Brigade, 1974), 56–57.

Chapter 10

1. Dietrich Bonhoeffer, *A Testament to Freedom: The Essential Writings of Dietrich Bonhoeffer,* ed Geffrey B. Kelly and F. Burton Nelson (San Francisco: HarperSanFrancisco, 1995), 206.

Chapter 21

1. Capelotti, P.J., *Our Man in the Crimea: Commander Hugo Koehler and the Russian Civil War* (Columbia: University of South Carolina Press, 1991), 4.

Chapter 23

1. Winston Churchill, "The Few," speech delivered August 20, 1940, House of Commons ("Winston S. Churchill Speeches and Quotes," The Churchill Centre: www.winstonchurchill.org).

2. Winston Churchill, "A House of Many Mansions," broadcast January 20, 1940 ("Winston S. Churchill Speeches and Quotes," The Churchill Centre: www.winstonchurchill.org).

Chapter 24

1. Pitcher, Harvey. *The Smiths of Moscow: A Story of Britons Abroad* (Cromer: Swallow House, 1984).

Chapter 25

1. Dietrich Bonhoeffer, *A Testament to Freedom: The Essential Writings of Dietrich Bonhoeffer,* ed Geffrey B. Kelly and F. Burton Nelson (San Francisco: HarperSanFrancisco, 1995), 279.

2. Victor Frankl, *Man's Search for Meaning* (Boston: Beacon, 2006), 134.

3. Dietrich Bonhoeffer, *Ethics* (Minneapolis: Fortress Press, 2001), 141.